# Contents

# Executive summary

## Introduction

- This research was designed to explore the perspective of family members on the coroner service, particularly the inquest, and to examine the views and experience of coroners and coroners officers.

- In conducting the research we observed a total of 81 inquests in nine coroners' districts. In 13 of these cases we interviewed members of the deceased's family. We also spoke at length to nine coroners, three deputy coroners, and 13 coroner's officers.

- In addition to the empirical investigation, we undertook a review of the legal framework within which the coroner service operates, including its relationship to other legal forums.

## The legal framework

- The criteria by which the coroner decides whether to investigate a death contain some ambiguity, most obviously in respect of the need to determine what constitutes an 'unnatural' death.

- The current law gives relatives few rights over the way the coroner's inquiry is conducted.

- The key question facing the inquest – how did the deceased come by his death? – can be answered on a number of different levels. Legislation and case law do not present a logical or coherent picture of what is required by way of answer to this question. There is no satisfactory explanation of what the inquest is looking for beyond the medical cause of death, and yet many recommended potential findings suggest that the inquest is intended to go further than this. There appear to be different interpretations of the question 'how did the deceased meet his death?' in different circumstances.

- There are numerous statements to the effect that the inquest is a fact-finding exercise and not a method of apportioning guilt or blame. Nonetheless, the inquest is often held to be a blaming institution by those who experience it.

- The inquest is inquisitorial rather than adversarial in character. This leaves coroners with effective control over which witnesses will be examined and what evidence will be presented. The role of 'properly interested persons' is limited; they cannot insist on particular witnesses being called, or particular evidence being produced. Also, it is nobody's legal responsibility to make sure that relatives are aware of their rights, or that they use those rights to best effect.

- 'Properly interested persons', including relatives, have the right to be represented at the inquest by a solicitor or barrister, but public funding is not available for legal representation at most inquests. There is no right of appeal against the inquest verdict such as exists in civil or criminal trials.

- When a person dies there is the possibility of a variety of legal proceedings. This requires rules to determine how one type of proceeding relates to another. It also raises questions about the purpose of holding inquests into deaths in respect of which other mechanisms are also being employed.

- The Human Rights Act 1998 may necessitate some changes to the existing legal structure, although it is not clear that such changes will be in the interests of the truth-seeking relative. This is because his or her interests may conflict with those of others who are involved in the inquest and whose rights also require to be protected.

## Relatives' experience of the coroner service

- On average there appeared to be a four to six months' interval between a person's death and the inquest, but a significant minority of inquests were subject to delays of at least a year. Delay in holding the inquest could be very distressing for relatives.

- The level of communication between the coroner service and families in the period leading up to the inquest varied considerably among districts. Most families appreciated the sympathetic treatment which they received from coroner's officers in this period; others were critical of what they perceived as poor liaison and a failure of care.

- Many family members were troubled by a realisation that they had not known what to expect from the inquest, and accordingly that they had been ill-prepared. Some regretted that they had not been consulted about the evidence to be gathered or about which witnesses should be called to give evidence. The absence of key witnesses made some inquests extremely disappointing and frustrating for relatives.

- Many coroners' courts are situated in rather run-down areas, and the geography of some older buildings can also appear unwelcoming. Location and venue have an influence upon families' experience of the inquest. These unfortunate first impressions could be overridden by the attitude of the coroners and the officers working in these buildings, but the level of care shown varied among courts.

- Many of the informants were anxious about the presence of reporters in the courtroom. The behaviour of some reporters showed scant respect for the feelings of family and friends.

- Inquests are often stressful occasions for those attending, and this could be exacerbated by tensions among those present. Quite often the physical positioning of family and witnesses within the courtroom added to these difficulties.

- Some of those attending found it difficult to comprehend the language of the courtroom, and this was exacerbated where the acoustics were poor, or where family members' first language was not English. It was apparent on several occasions that the family struggled to understand what was being said. Others lacked the education, or the assertiveness, to impose themselves on the inquest in order to have their questions answered. Some coroners were receptive to interventions from the floor of the court, even where these were poorly expressed or appeared barely relevant. Despite this, some families were effectively excluded from the inquiry.

- Despite these various difficulties, most families derived some benefit from the inquest. For some it helped to answer their questions, and many felt that the inquest acted as a memorial to the deceased.

## Selecting and presenting evidence

- Coroners vary considerably in their approach to calling witnesses to give oral evidence at the inquest. Sometimes the number of witnesses called could seem excessive, certainly if judged by reference to the coroner's need to compile sufficient evidence to arrive at a verdict; on the other hand, a failure to summon witnesses could result in the family being denied an opportunity to put questions on matters which were important to them.

- Coroners claimed, and we ourselves observed, that a willingness on the part of professional carers or medical staff to attend an inquest and explain in plain terms why the person had died was satisfying and reassuring to families.

- Sometimes a failure to summon witnesses compromised the declared objectives of the inquest. However, it was not necessarily easy to arrive at this judgement given the many different levels upon which it is possible to approach the 'how' question. Sometimes family members realised after the inquest was over that they had failed to take advantage of witnesses who were present in order to ask a question about something that was troubling them. This was less disturbing, however, than those occasions when someone whom the family had wished to question was simply not present.

- The course of the inquest can often seem predetermined – a parade of evidence (sometimes, not very much evidence) leading in a direction already decided by the coroner. By and large the inquest is not meant to be an occasion when there are any surprises, although new evidence could emerge in unexpected ways – for example, volunteered by members of the audience.

## Blame and adversarialism

- It is a curious feature of inquests that they will often devote considerable time and attention to matters that are quite explicitly beyond their remit. Many inquests had unacknowledged sub-texts, those sub-texts being of greater significance to some of the participants than the formally declared purposes of the hearing.

- Inquests were often focused upon the one issue which they are quite explicitly not meant to address – which is culpability. Many witnesses and observers were anxious to explore culpability. Coroners understood this, and they would allow interrogation of witnesses where this appeared to be the sole purpose. Despite this, the fiction was maintained that the inquest was not concerned with apportioning blame.

- Coroners were concerned, however, to avoid the kind of aggressive partisanship which is characteristic of criminal trials. So they would set limits upon questioning which was aimed at challenging, say, the quality of medical care. However, there is no clear definition of when this boundary has been reached, and no logical basis to determine when it *ought* to have been reached. This gave rise to some uncertainty, and to considerable disappointment on the part of some families.

## The verdict

- Some of the uncertainties and contradictions of the inquest are encapsulated in the relationship between evidence and verdict. It was routine for the evidence to be rehearsed in much more detail than was necessary in order to reach a verdict. In large part this seemed to be for the benefit of the family. Accordingly, there often appeared to be two distinct components of the inquest – the 'story' of the death and, secondly, the formal conclusion.

- In jury inquests the verdict tended to assume greater prominence. The presence of a jury meant that there was a stronger preoccupation with the decision which the jury would reach at the end of the day; much more than when the coroner was sitting alone, the verdict became the focus of the whole event.

- In order for a suicide verdict to be returned, the coroner (or the jury) has to be satisfied 'beyond reasonable doubt' – the criminal standard of proof. It was our impression that coroners set the 'bar' for a suicide verdict at a high level. As a result, it is likely that inquest verdicts understate the true level of suicide, although we recognise that erring on the side of caution may well be justified in the individual case.

- With road traffic accidents, on the other hand, there is seldom any question about the formal outcome. This suggests that the inquest is intended to fulfil some purpose other than simply to enable the coroner to reach a verdict.

## The overlap with other forums

- Coroners' powers are now considerably attenuated and an overlap has developed between their responsibilities and the responsibilities exercised in other forums, with the latter, generally speaking, having greater powers.

- One of the severest limitations upon the inquest emerged in cases where there was alleged criminal liability. The inquest hearing could be severely truncated in these circumstances, leading us to question its purpose.

- Where there were allegations of a failure of medical or other professional care, this could give rise to a suspicion that the inquest was being used as a dry run for a civil action for damages.

- Whilst coroners were prepared for, say, a hospital's procedure to be examined, they resisted the kind of full-blown adversarialism which characterises a civil action. Nonetheless, the character of the inquest was often influenced by the (unspoken) prospect of a claim for damages.

## What is it all for?

- The conduct of inquests is variable, depending on the circumstances and the approach of the individual coroner. The practice could not necessarily be predicted by reference to the inquest's declared purposes. In fact, whilst all inquests have some purposes in common, inquests are employed to serve a variety of *different* purposes.

- Difficulty arises because the inquest has travelled so far from its roots: in the great majority of cases there is no suggestion that the death is 'suspicious' – if by that is meant that the deceased may have been murdered.

- The question of which deaths need to be investigated by the coroner is troubling and complex. What is 'sudden' and what is 'suspicious'? There needs to be a more coherent and more comprehensive account of what the system is designed to achieve – and, following on from that, of which deaths need to be referred to the coroner, and under what circumstances the coroner needs to hold an inquest.

- Much of the difficulty in determining what the inquest is designed to achieve can be traced to the 'how' question. It is the layers of ambiguity surrounding this question, and the many levels upon which it can be answered, that lie behind the elusiveness and complexity of the inquest as a judicial forum.

- Both the research observations and subsequent interviews confirmed that the inquest can be an event of enormous symbolic significance for families. It can be a kind of epitaph – a final statement on someone's life and death. Other families had no such expectations, and it was not always easy for the coroner to predict what was expected of him/her.

- In some inquests it was hard to discern a legitimate public interest – which might argue for those hearings to be held in private (although the outcome could be made public).

## The future of the coroner service

- The fact that some relatives find the inquest to be of use in understanding or coming to terms with the death of the deceased, despite the fact that the family's welfare is not one of the inquest's stated aims, points to two possible alterations to the coroner's role. First, it leads to the question whether the welfare of relatives might be made a specific aim of the coroner's investigation and inquest. There are problems with incorporating such an aim, both in terms of drafting and in terms of possible conflict with the interests of witnesses and 'suspects'; the aim could, however, be qualified, being overridden when incompatible with the rights or interests of others. Secondly, this study suggests there is a strong case for greater standardisation of coroners' practice in the interests of family members.

- In considering reform it should be borne in mind that, imperfect and variable as the coroner system is in helping relatives to understand the events leading up to the death of a family member, it is, in many cases, the only mechanism which even attempts to do this. There are other forums in which a death may be discussed or investigated, but public inquiries will always be rare, and adversarial trials deal with issues of liability for specific wrongs, in which circumstance burdens of proof and the evidential 'rules of the game' operate to circumscribe the narrative of the death which emerges in court. It is only in the inquest that the deceased is the focus of the proceedings, rather than being a shadowy figure in somebody else's story.

- In addition to a review of the purposes of the inquest, there is a case for building more accountability into the system. There could be full-time coroners (probably quite few in number) who would be in charge of a region and who would act as superintending coroners, or as some sort of inspectorate; reporting to them would be individual coroners, part-time or full-time, depending on their jurisdiction or caseload.

- The relationship between coroners and coroner's officers is another area which might be looked at. Coroner's officers are not accountable to the coroner. Their line management is within the police service, but their police superior may be remote and with no influence over them. Their key working relationship is with the coroner, but in making this relationship work the coroner must rely on his *personal* attributes; s/he has no formal authority over these colleagues upon whom s/he must rely absolutely.

- It probably also makes sense to place responsibility for the coroners' jurisdiction at the door of just one government department. But institutional change will not of itself be an adequate response to the present confusions, uncertainties and overlaps which characterise the coroner service. The first task of any review must be to determine what exactly it is we expect of the coroner's inquiry and the inquest. From that, everything else follows.

# 1    Introduction

The coroner's inquiry is the state's immediate response to sudden or suspicious death. Most of the 190,000 or so deaths that are reported to coroners each year do not go to inquest; however, in some 13 per cent of these reported cases the coroner holds an inquest into the death[1]. This happens if, after a preliminary investigation, there is reason to suspect that the death was violent or unnatural; or it was of sudden and of unknown cause; or it occurred whilst the deceased was in custody (this includes deaths that occur in psychiatric institutions). When it is decided that a case should go to inquest, the coroner's office will inform next-of-kin and any witnesses to the death who may be required to give evidence. Prior to the inquest the coroner's office will prepare by obtaining statements from key witnesses. The coroner decides which of these witnesses will be required to give oral evidence at the inquest.

## The research focus

To date, the nature of the inquest and its relationship to other forums – for example, criminal proceedings, civil action for damages, or the public inquiry – have attracted little interest from socio-legal scholars. Also, little attention has been paid to the impact of the inquest upon family members and other witnesses – more specifically, the contribution which the inquest may make to helping families come to terms with their bereavement. It was the latter aspect which attracted the attention of Dr Tony Walter of the University of Reading, who was the instigator of this research project. His research proposal, delivered to the Home Office in March 2000, identified three research objectives, these being to discover:

- how bereaved people and witnesses experience the coroner service;
- how information provided by the coroner service helps interested parties to make sense of sudden death; and
- how the process helps witnesses deal with the burden of responsibility for a person's death.

Following the re-assignment of the research to Professor Gwynn Davis of the University of Bristol (in December 2000) a number of changes in the research design were agreed. The

---

1    Tarling, R. (1998) *Coroner Service Survey*, Home Office Research Study 181; London: The Home Office.

project would continue to explore the perspectives of family members, focusing upon their experience of the inquest. But it was proposed, in addition, to examine the inquest process in rather more detail by way of direct observation of a significantly greater number of inquests and, secondly, to attempt a more thorough-going examination of the views and experience of coroners and coroner's officers. So as well as exploring the perspectives of families, we were interested in the way coroners and coroner's officers perceived their various responsibilities, and any problems they had in discharging those.

Accordingly, our observation of inquests and our interviews with coroners and coroner's officers became key components of the study, with the material from those observations and those interviews being given equal weight alongside our interviews with representatives of families. By these means we have tried to understand the underlying purposes of the coroner's inquest, and also to explore whether these purposes may to some degree conflict.

We have also examined the relationship, and the overlap, between the coroner's inquest and other legal proceedings, both criminal and civil. This is relevant to the question of what the inquest is *for*, and thus the 'service' which coroners and their staff may be expected to offer families.

It has to be emphasised that the focus of the study was upon the inquest. We are not well placed to consider how bereaved relatives experience the coroner service in the 87 per cent of cases that do not result in an inquest. We talked to coroners and coroner's officers about every aspect of their work, but we gave limited attention to the decision whether or not to hold an inquest. So we cannot say, for example, whether this decision commonly gives rise to difficulty for coroners, or whether *not* holding an inquest creates dissatisfaction on the part of bereaved families. This focus upon the inquest inevitably limits the extent to which we can draw wider conclusions about coroners and the service they provide. Nonetheless, where we think it is justified we have used our empirical investigation as a means of exploring the underlying purposes of the coroner's investigation.

## The research team

The bulk of the fieldwork was undertaken by Dr Lindsey and Professor Davis. The research team was augmented by two other members of Bristol University Law Department – Dr Gwen Seabourne, who is a legal historian, and Dr Janine Griffiths-Baker, who is an expert in evidential matters. They commented on various draft reports, were responsible for Chapter 3 (see below), and also contributed to drafting our conclusions.

## Plan of the report

Chapter 2 gives a brief account of the research methods employed in undertaking the study, and the number of interviews and observations achieved. Chapter 3 summarises the legal framework within which the coroner service operates. It includes an account of the criteria for undertaking a coroner's investigation and holding an inquest; an examination of the role of the inquest; an exploration of the difficulties underlying the 'how' question; an explanation of the relationship of the inquest to other legal forums, including public enquiries; and an account of the legal rights of family members.

The next five chapters provide a thematic account of the evidence derived from our empirical investigation. Chapter 4 covers the preparation for the inquest; Chapter 5 reviews families' perception of their experience in the courtroom; Chapter 6 focuses upon coroners' selection and presentation of evidence; Chapter 7 addresses the theme of blame and adversarialism; and Chapter 8 is concerned with the verdict.

The final three chapters of the report are concerned with overarching themes or issues. Chapter 9 explores the overlap between the inquest and other legal forums. Chapter 10 reviews the underlying purposes of the inquest. Chapter 11 considers the future of the coronial system. This is followed by an Appendix containing a summarised account of 15 cases, including both observation of inquests and (where we achieved this) an account of our interview(s) with family members. We employ these cases for illustrative purposes in the body of the text.

# 2          Methodology

As noted in Chapter 1, this report contains an account, presented in Chapter 3, of the legal framework governing the coroners' inquiry and the inquest. That aside, this report is based on an empirical investigation, and in this chapter we summarise the methodology employed in the empirical component of our research. We include within the account of our fieldwork the inquests observed by Dr Tony Walter in autumn 2000.

## Observing inquests

We attended inquests in nine different coroners' districts, and in twelve coroners' courts. In all we observed a total of 81 individual inquests, these inquests being conducted by 13 different coroners or deputy coroners.

Our selection of inquests was determined simply by our wish to observe coroners' practice in these twelve different courts. We did not select inquests according to any particular criteria. Rather, our own availability determined which courts we would attend on which days.

## Interviews with family members

We asked coroners in seven districts to co-operate with us in approaching representatives of the families of the deceased. All seven coroners agreed to co-operate with the study.

From the 81 inquests that we observed, we selected 29 cases for follow-up (36% of the inquests attended). See Table 2.1 for a breakdown of the number of cases selected within each district.

Cases were selected for an approach to a member of the deceased's family if they had features of interest from a legal or sociological perspective; for example, where there were other legal proceedings in train, or where the status of next-of-kin was contested.

In respect of each of these cases selected for follow-up interview, we asked the coroner to write to a family member who had been present in court on the day of the inquest. The letter asked whether that person (or another family member) would be willing to be interviewed by a member of the research team.

- Forty-nine respondents were contacted from the 29 cases selected.
- Of these, 20 returned a reply slip (40%).
- Five of these respondents declined to be interviewed, but two sent letters briefly discussing the inquest and their reasons for refusal. These letters have been used as part of the dataset.
- One respondent sent a letter by e-mail, outlining some of the issues he wanted to bring to our attention.
- Out of the 29 cases in which approaches were made, we interviewed respondents in 13 cases, a success rate of 45 per cent.
- Eleven interviews were conducted face-to-face and two were conducted over the telephone.
- In all, 16 people were interviewed (including three members of one family and two members of another family).

Our respondents had mixed motives for agreeing to be interviewed. Some wanted to improve the system to make it more receptive to the needs of others who found themselves in their position. Others had a story to tell which they felt they had not been able to air fully at the inquest. Others used the interview as a way of talking through their feelings about the death of a family member or close friend.

We are committed to preserving the anonymity of everyone who helped us in this way. Accordingly, all names have been changed. It is still possible, we have no doubt, for family members to recognise themselves, but we consider that to be unavoidable and not, we hope, a breach of trust.

**Table 2.1:    Number of respondents contacted per court and rates of reply**

| Court | No. of inquests observed | No. of cases Chosen | No. of respondents contacted | No. of replies | No. of people interviewed | Face to face | Tel | Contact by letter |
|---|---|---|---|---|---|---|---|---|
| 1 | 8 | 1 | 3 | 1 | - | - | - | - |
| 2 | 16 | 4 | 8 | 5 | 2 | 2 | - | 2 |
| 3 | 1 | - | - | - | - | - | - | - |
| 4 | 3 | - | - | - | - | - | - | - |
| 5 | 7 | 3 | 4 | 1 | 1 | 1 | - | - |
| 6 | 5 | 3 | 6 | 1 | 1 | - | 1 | 1 |
| 7 | 2 | 2 | 2 | 1 | 2 | 2 | - | - |
| 8 | 10 | 8 | 15 | 5 | 3 | 2 | 1 | 1 |
| 9 | 4 | 2 | 2 | 1 | 3 | 3 | - | - |
| 10 | 13 | - | - | - | - | - | - | - |
| 11 | 4 | - | - | - | - | - | - | - |
| 12 | 8 | 6 | 9 | 5 | 4 | 4 | - | - |
| Totals | 81 | 29 | 49 | 20 | 16 | 14 | 2 | 4 |
| Total of negative replies | | | | 5 | | | | |
| Total who replied then lost contact | | | | 2 | | | | |

## Interviews with coroners and coroner's officers

We spoke at length to nine coroners and three deputy coroners about the inquest system and their role within it. Some coroners had several of these conversations with members of the research team.

We also interviewed 13 coroner's officers from nine districts. Again, we spoke to some of these coroner's officers on more than one occasion.

Dr Lindsey attended a Coroner's Officers Association conference in March 2001, and in the course of that conference had a number of informal conversations with coroner's officers from other districts. She has since had further contact with some of the coroner's officers that she met at the conference.

We do not refer to coroners by name, but employ an alphabetical suffix (for example, Coroner A). Two of the coroners whom we observed were female, but again with a view to preserving anonymity we refer to all coroners as 'he'. When we refer to coroner's officers we do not identify the district in which they were based.

## Acknowledgments

We should like to express our warm thanks to all those who took part in this study. We greatly appreciate the contribution of family members and friends of the deceased who agreed to talk to us at a very difficult time in their lives. We also appreciate the contribution of coroners and coroner's officers. The response to the study was unfailingly generous and we are grateful both for the time given and for the openness with which coroners and coroner's officers shared their experience and views.

# 3          The legal framework

The coroner service, as currently encountered by the relatives of deceased persons, is governed by rules to be found in a number of legal sources. The coroner's powers and duties are set out in a statute (the Coroners Act 1988) and secondary legislation (particularly the Coroners Rules 1984), both of which are supplemented and refined by case law[2]. It is therefore necessary to begin this chapter by examining the role and the rights which these sources accord to relatives of the deceased. It should be borne in mind that, since the coming into force of the Human Rights Act 1998, coroners' legislation must be interpreted in a manner compatible with the European Convention on Human Rights, and the coroner, as a 'public authority', must conduct himself or herself in a way which is not incompatible with individuals' rights under the Convention[3].

## Relatives and inquests: general points

The chapter will be devoted to a discussion of the legal role and rights of relatives with regard to coroners' investigations and inquests. Two matters must be noted at the outset. First, for the sake of simplicity the chapter is taking a fairly 'unified' view of relatives' desires, using as the paradigm a relative who is under no suspicion of criminal culpability or civil liability with respect to the death, and who wants as much of the truth to come out as is possible. It should, however, be borne in mind that in a number of cases a relative will be cast in the role of 'suspect' rather than truth-seeker, and so may have quite different desires and concerns. Secondly, turning to the legislation on coroners, it should be borne in mind that this does not specify that relatives form a particular category of people which an inquest seeks to benefit. The legislation does give them a greater role in the inquest process than most other members of the public, but the majority of their rights are not exclusive: similar rights are given to others who are regarded as 'properly interested persons'[4]. Their rights are also subject to a number of limitations, and there are areas in which families might expect to have some rights, but where in fact the current law grants them no rights, or limited rights.

---

2    Practice Notes for coroners are produced by the Coroners' Society, but have no direct legal force and are not generally available to the public.

3    See P. Jackson and P. Leopold, *O. Hood Phillips and Jackson, Constitutional and Administrative Law* (8th edn., London, 2001), chapter 22.

4    A 'proper interest' may be personal or financial, or may be the product of a legal obligation.

## Classification: which relatives are 'properly interested persons'?

The rights of relatives at the inquest are dependent on their being regarded as 'properly interested persons' by the coroner. The legislation, however, is unclear as to which relatives are to be regarded as 'properly interested', so coroners are left with a fairly wide discretion as to which people will be given this privileged status. Certain close family members – parents, spouses, children – are clearly 'properly interested'[5], but others – unmarried partners, siblings – will only be granted this status at the coroner's discretion[5]. We ourselves encountered few if any cases in which the privileged status of 'properly interested person' proved controversial, although it is always possible that people who would have liked to attend an inquest were not even aware of its being held.

It should also be noted that the rules on properly interested persons do not help in cases where there are disagreements within families, or complicated family situations. The difficult task of balancing different 'factions' is passed over in silence in the legislation, and also in all Home Office material and coroners' model charters. This can give rise to significant problems in practice, as our fieldwork demonstrates.

## Criteria for coroner investigation/inquest

Relatives of a deceased person have very little control over whether or not a coroner decides to investigate the death. Relatives' consent is not required for a coroner's inquest or post mortem. Even in the case of the parents of deceased children, there is no power to refuse permission either to investigate or to hold an inquest[7]. Similarly, relatives have no power to compel a coroner to investigate or hold an inquest[8]. The decision as to whether or not to become involved is for the coroner to make, in accordance with his or her duties under the law. Under current law a coroner must hold an inquest when informed that a body is within his/her district and "there is reasonable cause to suspect that the deceased:

a) has died a violent or an unnatural death;
b) has died a sudden death of which the cause is unknown; or
c) has died in prison or in such a place or in such circumstances as to require an inquest under any other Act[9]."

5   CR rr. 20 (2)(a)-(g).
6   CR r. 20(2)(h).
7   CA 1988 s.8; *Jervis*, 10-23.
8   There is in fact provision to seek an order from the High Court to require an inquest to be held in circumstances where a coroner has neglected or refused to hold one (CA 1988 s.13).
9   CA 1988 s.8 (1).

These criteria are not free from ambiguity. It is not immediately obvious which deaths are 'violent', 'unnatural' or 'sudden'. The 'unnaturalness' criterion is a particular problem. This may be seen in the context of potential medical negligence cases. Some cases in which relatives suspect that negligence caused or contributed to the death of the deceased may be weeded out because the death is held by a coroner not to be 'unnatural'[10].

Lawyers have expressed some disquiet about the complexity and ambiguity of the rules governing the circumstances in which inquests should be held[11], presumably with a view to making it easier to challenge coronial decisions on this issue. There is, however, a view which goes in the opposite direction as to the correct legislative strategy, suggesting that there should be a greater scope for coronial discretion (coupled with a reduction in the number of categories of deaths which coroners are obliged to investigate)[12]. If the latter strategy were adopted, this would no doubt be seen as contrary to the interests of the truth-seeking relative, but it might avoid what are arguably unnecessary inquests into certain categories of death, thus saving some bereaved relatives the delay and distress associated with an inquest.

## The legal rights of relatives before an inquest

### Treatment of the body

The current law gives relatives few rights with respect to the way in which the body of the deceased is treated before it is released to them for the funeral. If a post mortem examination is to be held, relatives have limited influence over the selection of a doctor to carry it out[13]. They have no control over the nature of the examination.

10  In. *R v Poplar Coroner ex p. Thomas* [1993] 2 WLR 547, for example, a 17 year old girl who was asthmatic had a severe attack. An ambulance was called and arrived 33 minutes late. The girl died in hospital, and there was evidence that she would not have died if she had arrived at hospital earlier. The coroner held that this was not an unnatural death, even if the late arrival of the ambulance was negligent, because asthma is a natural condition, so there was no need for an inquest. The Court of Appeal in this case held that 'unnatural' is an ordinary English word, so "it was for the coroner to say, within certain limits of tolerance, whether the death was 'unnatural', and on the evidence, he was entitled to conclude that it was so" *Jervis*, 8-20.
See also *R v Inner London Coroner, ex p. Touche* [2001] 2 All ER 752, which concerned the decision by a coroner not to hold an inquest because he regarded a death as not being 'unnatural'. The deceased died after having a Caesarean section in a (private) hospital. There were questions about her treatment after the operation. She died from a cerebral haemorrhage eight days later. Her husband wanted an inquest to be held and the Court of Appeal agreed that an inquest ought to be held, as there was reasonable cause to suspect that the death was at least contributed to by neglect, which, they decided, made it 'unnatural'. Although the decision that there should be an inquest in this case may be sensible, it is not obvious that one can reach the desired result by using the 'unnaturalness' criterion.
11  APIL (Association of Personal Injury Lawyers) – Association of Personal Injury Lawyers 6 Feb. 2001.
12  "Mandatory inquests should be abolished, except for deaths in custody or accidents at work, and greater discretion given to coroners". Pounder, 1502.
13  Coroners Act 1988 s. 21(3).

It has been suggested that some decisions by coroners as to treatment of the body could be subject to objection under the provisions of the Human Rights Act 1998. The provisions which might be applicable are the rights to respect for privacy and family life (article 8) and freedom of thought, conscience and religion (article 9). These rights might be cited in cases where there is religious objection to disruption of bodily integrity or delayed burial. It seems unlikely that these rights would be allowed to prevail over the legitimate state interest in investigating deaths, but it is possible that there will be legal challenges to some coroners' decisions based on these grounds[14]. It should also be noted that the limited nature of the inquest means that it will not explore any irregularities or lack of respect or sensitivity in the handling of the body of the deceased after death[15].

It is not clear that a coroner is obliged to allow or assist relatives to view the body: certainly there is no such provision in the coroners legislation[16], but it has been suggested that article 8 of the Human Rights Convention (right to respect for family life, home and correspondence) might now afford relatives a right to view the body[17]. It has been suggested that, in order to remove any doubt, there should be a statutory right for victims' relatives to view the body immediately, even if it is disfigured or decomposed[18], and that facilities for viewing bodies whilst they are in the mortuary, in the legal possession of the coroner, should be made available[19].

## Information

Under current coroners legislation, relatives' legal right to be notified of a coroner's investigation, post mortem or inquest is limited. In the case of a post mortem, coroners have an obligation to inform relatives of the time and place of the examination only if they have notified the coroner that they wish to attend or be represented at the examination. The coroner is not obliged to notify them even then if it is impracticable or to do so would cause

14 Pounder, 'The coroner service, a relic in need of reform', 1999 *British Medical Journal* 318, 1502-3.

15 See, on this point, our note on Inquest 9 in the Appendix to this report. The relatives of the Marchioness victims were particularly unhappy about the treatment of the bodies of deceased relatives. There were clearly some actions which were taken without considering the feelings of relatives, but they were not contrary to the law relating to coroners. Dr Knapman was criticised by Lord Justice Clarke for failing to give instruction that hands should be reunited with bodies. *Pl*, 12.8. One set of hands was found in 1993 in the mortuary freezer, and destroyed, on the instructions of Dr Knapman: *Pl*, 7.7. The Marchioness Action group's spokeswoman saw this unjustified removal and retention of hands as contrary to the human rights of relatives. *The Guardian*, 23 March, 2001.

16 There was some unhappiness amongst the relatives of victims of the Marchioness disaster that they had been barred, or at least dissuaded, from viewing the bodies of their relatives 'for their own good' when these were damaged or disfigured.

17 *Pl*, 23.1.

18 *The Times* 24 March 2001.

19 *Pl*, 23.2-5; 29.38.

the examination to be unduly delayed[20]. If an inquest is to be held, notice must be given to any spouse, relative or personal representative of the deceased whose name and address are known to the coroner, and to any properly interested person who has asked the coroner for notification of the time and place of the inquest and has supplied a telephone number or address for the purpose of being so notified[21]. The onus is therefore on relatives to contact the coroner, rather than on the coroner to find the relatives and inform them. If relatives are not informed by the coroner that an inquest will be held, they may not find out about it since "it is desirable, but not a legal necessity, that due public notice of the holding of an inquest should be given"[22]. It is possible that the lack of a requirement for information to be provided to relatives may be challenged as contrary to Article 8 of the European Convention on Human Rights[23]. It was a recurring theme in our interviews with relatives, reported in succeeding chapters, that some of them felt ill-informed in respect of the procedures to be adopted at the inquest.

### Timing

The legislation makes specific mention of arranging inquests so as not to inconvenience jurors or witnesses, but relatives are not specifically mentioned[24]. There is no provision regarding the time within which an inquest must be held. Our study revealed that inquests are commonly not held until many months – even a year or more – after the death.

## The decision as to whether or not a jury will be used

Coroners' inquests may be held with or without a jury. The decision as to whether or not to use a jury is, once again, one for the coroner to make, in accordance with the law. There is no role for relatives in deciding whether to proceed with or without a jury[25].

The circumstances under which a jury should, or may, be used are set out in the legislation. A coroner must use a jury if "it appears to [him/her] that there is reason to suspect:

    (a) that the death occurred in prison or in such a place or in such circumstances as to require an inquest under any other Act;

---

20  CR r. 7(1).
21  *Jervis*, 10-08, CR r 19.
22  *Jervis*, 10-07.
23  Friedman, D. (2001) 'The Human Rights Act and the Inquest Process', *Legal Action*, part 2, 17.
24  *Jervis*, 10-01, CA s.14.
25  CA 1988 s.8; *Jervis*, 10-23.

(b) that the death occurred while the deceased was in police custody, or resulted from an injury caused by a police officer in the purported execution of his duty;

(c) that the death was caused by an accident, poisoning or disease, notice of which is required to be given under any Act;

(d) that the death occurred in circumstances the continuance or possible recurrence of which is prejudicial to the health or safety of the public or any section of the public[26]."

Subsections (a)–(c) are clear in their application, but subsection (d) leaves a large amount of discretion to the coroner and is likely to lead to inconsistent practice.

Whether or not the law as to when a jury is to be used is unfavourable to relatives depends on whether inquests with juries are better mechanisms for bringing out the true circumstances of the death than are inquests with coroners alone. It might be conjectured that relatives will get more out of an inquest with a jury than an inquest before a coroner alone, since (a) more evidence would have to be presented at the jury inquest in order to allow the jury to make a decision when coming to the facts 'from scratch', whereas a coroner sitting alone will have informed him/herself of the basic facts before the inquest; and (b) evidence at a jury inquest will have to be presented in a simple way in order to make sure that the jury follows it, which might make it more easily comprehensible to some relatives.

## The functions of the inquest

It is frequently suggested that there is something of a conflict between the purpose of the inquest and the wish of many relatives to use it to apportion blame for a death[27]. Relatives may be surprised or frustrated with some of the legal limitations on the scope of the inquest.

According to the law, the inquest is an inquiry intended to produce a formal answer (in so far as it is possible) to four questions:

---

26  CA s.8(3).
27  *Jervis*, 12-101; CR r.36; CA s.11(3); *R v North Humberside Coroner ex p. Jamieson* [1994] 3 WLR 82: P. Matthews, 'What is the Coroner For?' 110 LQR (1994) 536, 537: "[I]n very many cases, the deceased's family and friends may seek to push the inquiry ... to the point where some imputation of responsibility or blame can be made. Many inquests are battlegrounds more bitter than any litigation. For one thing, they take place much sooner after the death than any civil action would, when feelings are still running high. For another, the family or friends usually have no information provided to them in advance of the hearing as to what will be said by any of the witnesses (or indeed which witnesses will be called. This state of ignorance is shared by all the other 'interested persons'..., but in the case of family and friends it often fuels mistrust, and sometimes creates suspicion of a cover up."

(i) who the deceased was;

(ii) when he 'came by his death';

(iii) where he 'came by his death'[28]; and

(iv how he 'came by his death'.

Three of these questions are relatively straightforward, but the question of 'how the deceased came by his death' can be answered at a number of different levels. It could be taken to mean 'What did the deceased and others do in the moments leading up to the death?' or 'What were the physical processes leading to death?' or 'Whose fault was the death?' It could be argued that legislation, case law and other pronouncements on the inquest do not present a logical or coherent picture of what is required by way of answer to this question. A leaflet from the Home Office states that the inquest looks for 'the medical cause of death'[29], but some of the recommended findings for inquests – natural causes; industrial disease; dependence on drugs/ non-dependent abuse of drugs; want of attention at birth; suicide; attempted/ self-induced abortion; accident/misadventure; sentence of death; lawful killing; open verdict; unlawful killing; stillbirth; (with the possibility that the first four conclusions may be qualified as being 'aggravated' by lack of care or self-neglect)[30] – suggest that the inquest is looking for something more than this. Whether a killing is lawful or unlawful, for example, is hardly something which could be described as 'the medical cause of death'.

There is, however. no satisfactory explanation of exactly what it is that the inquest is looking for beyond the medical cause of death. An accurate but ultimately question-begging statement is that by Lord Lane CJ in *R. v South London Coroner ex p. Thompson*: "The function of an inquest is to seek out and record as many of the facts concerning the death as public interest requires"[31]. The Court of Appeal in *ex p. Jamieson* substituted one ambiguous phrase for another, regarding "how the deceased came by his death" as an inquiry into "the means by which the deceased came by his death"[32]. That case concerned a death by self-hanging in prison, and, whereas it might make sense in these circumstances to reformulate the 'how' question to ask 'by what means' the deceased died, that formulation would not be a good one for other sets of facts, and certainly does not represent everything which coroners are prepared to consider in their actual practice.

The ambiguity of the 'how' question can only be understood by considering the history of the inquest, an institution which has existed at least since the late twelfth century. In origin

28 CA s.11(5).

29 HO leaflet *When sudden death occurs, coroners and inquests* www.homeoffice.gov.uk/ccpd/sdndh00.html, 2.

30 CR Sched. 4 form 22: P. Matthews and J. Foreman (eds), *Jervis on the Office and Duties of Coroners*, 11th ed, (London, 1993), 13-16.

31 (1982) 126 S.J. 625: *Jervis*, 1-08.

32 *R v North Humberside Coroner ex p. Jamieson* [1995] QB 1.

the inquest into deaths regarded as suspicious or otherwise of concern to the crown was important as a method of detecting foul play and in initiating prosecution of suspects. It was certainly looking at 'how the deceased died' in the sense of 'who or what was to blame'. However, the inquest's role in the detection and prosecution of crime has been superseded by the development of new institutions (the police force, state prosecution, other forms of inquiry), and also deliberately diminished because of a perceived incompatibility with the rights of those who may be either accused of crime or subject to a civil action[33].

The limitations placed on the 'how' question mean that there is no longer a single, coherent explanation of what is being sought. Arguably, there are different interpretations of the question 'how did the deceased meet his death?' in different types of inquest. In the case of a suspected suicide, for example, 'how did the deceased meet his death?' comes close to meaning 'did the deceased intentionally take his own life?' In other words, the inquest will explore who was *responsible* for the death – either the deceased or somebody else. However, in the case of a death on the operating table, coroners are required to steer the inquest away from apportioning responsibility or blame. A recent report by the New Zealand Law Commission recognises that the coroner's inquest is asking different versions of the 'how' question in inquests into different sorts of death[34].

Approaching the 'how' question from a different angle, it is clear that matters which on some interpretations might be part of an inquiry into how a person died are stated not to be part of the inquest. In particular, inquests are not supposed to make findings about criminal or civil responsibility for a death[35]. A relative or anyone else seeking to use an inquest to blame an identified, living individual for a death, will be restrained from doing so[36]. Dillon LJ, in *R v Poplar Coroner's Court ex p. Thomas*, noted that "it is not the function of a coroner's inquest to provide a forum for attempts to gather evidence for pending or future criminal or civil proceedings"[37]. There are numerous statements to the effect that "an inquest is a fact finding exercise and not a method of apportioning guilt"[38].

It should, however, be noted that, despite these limitations, some people find that the inquest can be a blaming institution, as can be seen by cases brought by those who feel

---

33  For a summary of twentieth century evolution of the coroner's role, see *R v North Humberside Coroner ex p. Jamieson* [1994] 972 at 977-81. For a recent discussion of the 'how' question in the context of human rights, see the opinion of Sir Stephen Sedley in *Keenan v UK* BHRC 319, para. 9, cited in Friedman, 34.

34  New Zealand Law Commission Preliminary Paper 36, *Coroners: A Review* (1999), p.2.

35  CR r.42.

36  *R v South London Coroner, ex p. Thompson* (1982) 126 SJ 625.

37  [1993] 2 WLR 547 at 553; *Jervis*, 1-08.

38  Lord Lane CJ in *R v South London Coroner ex p. Thompson* [1982] 126 SJ 625, *Jervis*, 1-07. There is a suggestion that the Human Rights Act 1998 s. 3 may be used to challenge restrictions on the 'how' question with regard to culpability issues, at least in cases involving deaths in custody: see Friedman, part 2, 16.

that they have been held to be at fault in inquests[39]. There also seems to be considerable variation among coroners in the degree to which they will allow issues of culpability to be aired.

## The inquest

### Attendance, publicity
As inquests are public, there are no restrictions on relatives attending. This also means, however, that even in cases which relatives may find painful or embarrassing, they have no right to ask for the inquest to be held in private: inquests must be held in public unless national security dictates otherwise[40].

### Relatives' participation in the inquest
An inquest differs from other proceedings in England and Wales (such as a civil or criminal trial) in that it is inquisitorial rather than adversarial in nature[41]. In contrast to the manner in which adversarial trials are conducted, there are no parties who present their respective viewpoints to a judge sitting as an impartial umpire. In an inquest it is the coroner who takes the initiative in conducting the case. He (or she) leads the investigation, decides which evidence and witnesses will be called, examines the evidence, and questions the witnesses. Decisions as to which evidence will be included are for the coroner. The Coroners Act 1988 provides that:

> The coroner shall ... examine on oath concerning the death all persons who tender evidence as to the facts of the death and all persons having knowledge of those facts whom he considers it expedient to examine[42].

This leaves coroners with effective control over which witnesses will be examined, and what evidence will be presented at the inquest.

The coroner has the power to admit documentary evidence, by way of written statement by any witness, if he is of the view that such evidence is likely to be undisputed[43]. There is no right of discovery (compelling others to give access to material before proceedings) in

39  See, e.g., *R v HM Coroner for Coventry ex p. Chief Constable of Staffordshire Police* (2000) 164 JP 665.
40  CR r. 17; *Jervis*, 10-23.
41  *R v South London Coroner, ex p. Thompson* (1982) 126 SJ 625.
42  CA s. 11(2).
43  CR r. 37(1).

relation to evidence which coroners have gathered for a inquest[44]. *Jervis*, however, notes that "the coroner may exceptionally decide to disclose the substance of important documentary evidence (e.g. a suicide note) to interested persons before the inquest, but it is a matter for him"[45]. It is suggested that relatives may be entitled to disclosure under the Human Rights Act 1998 and European Convention on Human Rights[46].

Some concession is made to the fact that certain people, particularly relatives, have a greater interest in the investigation and its outcome than do other members of the public, and they are given some privileges and opportunities to participate in the inquest. 'Properly interested persons' may examine witnesses either in person or through their legal representative[47]. Ultimate control, however, remains with the coroner. It is s/he who decides whether a person wishing to participate in the inquest in this way is to be classed as an 'interested person'.

At the inquest, witnesses must be examined by the coroner before any properly interested person may examine them[48]. The role of 'interested persons' is limited. They cannot insist on particular witnesses being called, or particular evidence being produced[49], but the coroner must consider any applications made by such 'interested persons' to call particular witnesses or to request additional documentation[50]. Relatives may challenge a decision not to call particular witnesses on the ground that the coroner's investigation has been inadequate[51]. Relatives and other 'properly interested persons' may examine witnesses either personally (if necessary, with the help of the coroner in formulating the questions) or through a legal representative[52].

In cases where a person wishes to examine witnesses, but the coroner decides that s/he is not a properly interested person, it has proved difficult to challenge the coroner's decision. In one case the brother of the deceased was held not to be properly interested for this purpose, and this was upheld on appeal[53]. It is, however, possible that the Human Rights Act 1998 will make a difference here, allowing relatives to mount a successful challenge[54].

---

44  *Jervis*, 10-37, *R v Southwark Coroner ex p. Hicks* [1987] 1 WLR 1624.
45  *Jervis*, 10-37.
46  Friedman, part 2, 18.
47  CR r.20.
48  CR r.21.
49  CR rr 19(b), 2(2)(e); *Jervis*, 10-11.
50  *Jervis*, 12-60.
51  *Jervis*, 10-13.
52  CR r.20; *Jervis*, 11-05; *Jervis*, 12-97.
53  *R v Portsmouth Coroner ex p. Keane* (1989) 153 JP, 658, 661. In another case, a coroner had ruled that two sisters were not 'properly interested persons' at their brother's inquest, although in this case, the decision was overruled – *R v South London Coroner ex p. Driscoll* (1993) 159 JP 45.
54  Friedman, part 2, 17.

Relatives' right to ask questions may be rendered less valuable by the fact that they are not always told in advance of their right to do this. There is no obligation on coroners to tell relatives that they may ask questions: a coroner does not have the obligations that a judge in a civil case has towards a litigant in person. It is nobody's legal responsibility to make sure that relatives are aware of their rights, or that they use them to their best effect. Likewise, there is no provision requiring facilities for relatives with a poor grasp of English.

When an 'interested person' is examining a witness, the coroner once again retains ultimate control. S/he has the power to disallow irrelevant questions or those which transgress other rules[55]. One important respect in which questions may be improper is when they tend to 'widen the coroner's inquest into adversarial fields of conflict'[56]. Jervis also suggests that intrusive questions and 'questions which are in fact attempts to air views, rather than to elicit facts surrounding the death' are improper[57].

Because the general rules of evidence in English law have developed in the adversarial context, they are not necessarily appropriate to the inquisitorial forum of the coroner's inquest. One commentator has observed that "the wholly inquisitorial procedure before a coroner is inimical to the application of the rules of evidence, which accordingly do not apply to such proceedings"[58]. The practical result is that evidence and questions will not necessarily be disallowed because they fall within one of the categories excluded in criminal or civil trials, such as hearsay evidence or leading questions.

The coroner, then, is generally in control of the evidence at an inquest. There is, however, one important way in which others may have the final say as to whether or not a particular line of questioning will be allowed. Even if a question is relevant and not otherwise open to objection, a witness can claim the privilege against self-incrimination to refuse to answer questions which might tend to expose him or her to criminal prosecution, but not those which might expose him or her to civil suit[59]. See, for example, Inquest 8 in the Appendix.

---

55  *Jervis*, 11-08, CR r 20(1) (a); *Jervis*, 12-99, CR r.20(1)(b).
56  *Jervis*, 12-08; Griffiths J in *R v Hammersmith Coroner ex p.* Peach [1980] QB 211, 220.
57  *Jervis*, 12-103 (no authority cited).
58  *Cross and Tapper on Evidence* (9th edition) p.20. See also, *R v West London Coroner, ex p. Gray* [1988] QB 467; *Mckerr v Armagh Coroner* [1990] 1 All ER 865. Although not bound by the strict rules of evidence, however, *Jervis* states that it is "desirable for coroners to be aware of the main rules of evidence, so as to reduce so far as possible the number of occasions upon which it is necessary to depart from them": *Jervis*, 12-111.
59  *Jervis*, 12-129.

## Legal representation

'Properly interested persons', including relatives, have the right to be represented at the inquest by a solicitor or barrister, but, although public funding may be available for 'legal advice and assistance falling short of taking any step in proceedings or representing a person', it is not available for legal representation at the inquest[60]. There have been calls for greater availability of public funding for representation at inquests[61], as the rights of 'properly interested persons' who are unrepresented may be rendered nugatory if they are not personally capable of formulating useful questions and putting them to witnesses.

## The outcome

Once all the evidence has been received, the coroner (if sitting with a jury) must sum up and give directions on all points of law raised by the case[62]. The coroner or jury will then consider their verdict. The verdict should answer the questions as to who the deceased was, and how, when and where he met his death[63]. In answering 'how' the deceased died, the Coroners Rules 1984[64] give a list of suggested (but not compulsory) conclusions:

> natural causes;
> industrial disease;
> dependence on drugs/non-dependent abuse of drugs;
> want of attention at birth;
> suicide;
> attempted/self-induced abortion;
> accident/misadventure;
> sentence of death;
> lawful killing;

---

60  *Jervis*, 10-35.

61  Note that the Stephen Lawrence inquiry recommended considering a change in this rule: P. Matthews, 'Coroners' Inquests and the Stephen Lawrence Inquiry', (1999) 149 *NLJ*, 418, and note the author's concern that public funding might turn the inquest into a 'prosecution manqué' – p. 418. Matthews also states that there is a great deal of free representation by lawyers at inquests – p.419. A representative of the Association of Personal Injury Lawyers (a professional body which seeks to promote the seeking of compensation for negligence), Patrick Allen, suggested that legal aid should be available to bereaved families for inquests. AP 119/2 April 2001. The organisation INQUEST, which is concerned with deaths in custody and their investigation, also recommends that public funding should be available: http://www.inquest.org.uk. The Lord Chancellor's Department has recently taken steps to make public funding available for representation at, mainly, inquests into deaths in custody.

62  CR r. 41.

63  CA s. 11(5)(a).

64  Schedule 4, Form 22.

open verdict;
unlawful killing; and
still birth.

An open verdict should be recorded if any of the other suggested conclusions could not be proven.

The standard of proof required is usually the 'civil standard' – i.e. the jury or the coroner must be satisfied 'on the balance of probabilities' that the death happened in a particular manner. In the case of conclusions of suicide and unlawful killing, however, greater certainty is required. The law requires that these conclusions should not be reached unless the 'criminal standard of proof' (beyond reasonable doubt) is met[65]. As we discovered, coroners' practice seems to be even more lenient than the law requires, with what seem virtually certain to have been suicides made the subject of open verdicts.

## After the inquest

### *Information*
The coroner must supply copies of any post mortem report to 'properly interested persons', provided they apply to the coroner and pay the prescribed fee. Alternatively, they may be permitted to inspect the report without charge[66]. The coroner has no obligation to inform relatives of the outcome of the inquest[67]. The Home Office, however, recommends that the coroner should normally ensure that an appropriate person should be made aware of the results of the inquest[68].

The Alder Hey Report criticises the lack of information given to parents following investigations (in this case post mortems) by the coroner[69]. It has been suggested that more and better information should be provided for relatives at every stage of a coroner's investigation and/or inquest[70].

65  *R v Newbury Coroner, ex p. John* (1991) 156 JP 456. This is despite the fact that suicide is no longer a crime and so, arguably, a suicide verdict could be reached 'on the balance of probabilities' as with other verdicts.
66  CR 57.
67  *Jervis*, 18-24.
68  HO Circular no. 53 of 1980.
69  *AHR* p.23, 3.5.
70  *PI*, 4.3. PI, 29.41; *AHR* p.69. 7.1; p.338, 29; p.339-40, 33.1; p.340, 34.1; p.354, 56; *AHR* p.353, 55.

## Challenging the coroner's decisions

There is no right of appeal against the inquest verdict such as exists in civil or criminal trials. Relatives can, however, challenge the outcome on grounds that the conclusion was reached without attention to relevant matters, or that it is unreasonable. There are two legal routes for them to do this: (a) under a specific procedure in s.13 of the Coroners Act 1988; (b) by applying for judicial review[71]. If successful in such legal action, the coroner may be ordered to investigate, or the inquest may be quashed. However, it is often difficult to show that a coroner ought to have investigated a death where s/he refused to do so, or should not have investigated a death though s/he did so. This is a result of the vagueness of the criteria for investigation (e.g. the 'unnaturalness' criterion, mentioned above)[72] and the case law on this matter which has rendered coroners' decisions on whether or not to investigate virtually unchallengeable unless they are completely unreasonable[73]. The new, more interventionist 'human rights orientated judicial review' may, however, allow dissatisfied relatives more chance of a successful challenge[74].

## The relationship between inquests and other proceedings

When a person dies there is the possibility of legal proceedings other than a coroner's inquest. Depending on the circumstances of the death, there may be a criminal or a civil trial, professional proceedings, a public inquiry, or other statutory inquiry. In potential medical negligence cases, for example, a complaint may be made to the General Medical Council or to a medical ombudsman. Alternatively, a negligence suit may be brought. Similarly, in potential homicide cases a criminal prosecution or a civil suit may likewise be pursued. In addition, there is in all cases the possibility of a public inquiry[75]. The existence of a variety of legal mechanisms which might be brought into play to investigate the circumstances of a death necessitates rules as to how one type of proceeding relates to another. It also raises questions about the purpose of inquests into certain deaths in respect of which other mechanisms are also employed.

71  CPR Sch.1, RSC Order 53.

72  *Jervis*, c.5.

73  See, e.g., *Terry v East Sussex Coroner* [2001] 3 WLR 605. A professional body representing lawyers who work in the field of personal injury law recently suggested that there should be improved provision for appeal against coroners' decisions, or result of the inquest: APIL wants families of deceased persons to "have access to a simple, direct, appeals procedure if they are not satisfied" – AP116 Feb. 2001.

74  See *Secretary of State for the Home Department ex p.Daly* [2001] UKHL 26, cited in Friedman, part 2, 17.

75  On public inquiries, see A.W. Bradley and K.D. Ewing, *Constitutional and Administrative Law* (12th edn., London, 1998) 753-6.. Public inquiries may be instituted under a variety of powers, e.g. the Alder Hey inquiry was an Independent Confidential Inquiry under s.2 of the National Health Service Act 1977: *AHR* p.5, 2.1. It had the duty to "make and direct all necessary searching investigations and to produce the witnesses in order to arrive at the truth" in accordance with The Royal Commission on Tribunals of Inquiry (CMND 3121 1966 paragraph 28) [p.6, 6.3].

In contrast to their former crucial role in the investigation of crime and commencement of criminal prosecutions, inquests are now marginalised in potential serious crime cases. If someone is charged with murder, manslaughter or infanticide, a road traffic offence involving death, an offence related to suicide, or another offence connected with the death of the deceased, the inquest must usually be adjourned. If resumed, it must not give a finding inconsistent with the criminal proceedings[76]. This brings into question the purpose of holding an inquest in such cases[77].

Although there is no bar to holding an inquest and having civil proceedings based on the same facts, questions may also arise as to the need, or the benefit, of holding an inquest in these circumstances. From the perspective of a relative who is planning to bring a civil suit in connection with the death of the deceased, some benefit may be derived from the (relative) speed with which an inquest can be convened. Medical negligence cases take some time to come to court and even though recent reforms may have improved matters, an inquest should still be much quicker. A second possible advantage arises from the fact that as a great many medical negligence cases eventually settle, an inquest is likely to generate more publicity, thereby highlighting issues of public concern.

Public inquiries and inquests may also overlap. Again, inquests should have the advantage of speed, and resource implications mean that public inquiries will never be able to replace inquests. However, in cases where there is both an inquest and a public inquiry relating to the same death, public inquiries have certain important advantages for relatives. In particular, public inquiries have a broader remit than the limited questions to be answered at an inquest. They are also able to explore issues of culpability. They are usually headed by a judge or barrister and, unlike an inquest, the parties are represented by lawyers who question the witnesses. The other side of the coin, as far as relatives are concerned, is that the quasi-adversarial nature of most inquiries means that if a line of inquiry is not in the interests of any of the parties, it may not be followed. Inquests, on the other hand, are not concluded until all the evidence has been heard. This may assist relatives in deciding whether to pursue a civil claim.

Relatives (or their lawyers) may want evidence gathered for the purposes of the inquest to be made available for use in other proceedings. There are, however, limits as to the way in which inquest evidence may be used in adversarial proceedings. Inquest findings do not

76  *Jervis*, 12-39, CA 1988 s. 16(7).

77  The resumed inquest into the death of Stephen Lawrence illustrates some of the problems which may occur in such circumstances, particularly when criminal prosecutions have failed. In such a case, relatives may be particularly keen to go beyond the remit of the inquest and deal with issues of culpability and negligence, but the limitations of the inquest mean that they are unlikely to find it satisfying: *Lawrence* chapter 42.

bind any person affected by them (in civil or criminal law)[78], nor is the record of evidence at the inquest admissible as evidence of the facts which they state, although it may be used as the basis for cross-examination in a subsequent trial[79]. The Association of Personal Injury Lawyers has called for a change in evidential rules to allow inquest verdicts to be relied on in negligence cases, "to prevent bereaved families from enduring long, drawn-out and unnecessary proceedings"[80].

## Conclusion

Relatives have a number of rights with respect to the inquest process, but these rights are limited by legal provisions, by the existence of a wide discretion exercised by the coroner (exercise of which will be difficult to challenge), by the fact that financial assistance is not usually available for legal representation, and by the weak or non-existent requirement for relatives to be informed of events or to be advised of their rights. It is probably not surprising, and is not illogical, that relatives' rights should be limited, given that helping relatives is not and never has been a specific objective of the legal framework for inquests. Furthermore, relatives' needs and wishes may conflict with those of others (especially other witnesses). The Human Rights Act 1998 may necessitate some changes in the existing legal structure, though it is not clear that any such changes will be in the interests of the truth-seeking relative. Again, this is because his or her interests may clash with those of others involved in the inquest whose rights also require to be protected[81].

---

78  *Jervis*, 20-02.
79  *Jervis*, 20-06.
80  APIL 6 February. 2001.
81  Friedman, part 2, 16-21. Friedman suggests that the rights of relatives with respect to inquests may be enhanced by use of article 2 (right to life) and article 3 (prohibition on inhuman and degrading treatment) and the interpretation which case law has given these provisions. Some of these rights, however, are likely to conflict with rights of 'suspect-witnesses' at inquests, who may rely on their right to a fair trial.

# 4          Preparing for the inquest

"The importance of thorough preparation before an inquest cannot be overemphasised[82]."

When a coroner decides that an inquest is necessary, he will instruct his officers to collect the various statements and reports bearing on that case. As part of this process there will be contact with the deceased's next-of-kin and, in addition to any statements which may be required of them, they will be informed of the date of the inquest. In this chapter we draw on our observation of inquests and our interviews with family members in order to reflect upon this preparation process.

## Timing

There is no specific time period within which an inquest must be held following a death[83]. It seemed from our observations that on average there was a four to six month interval between the person's death and the inquest. However, this time period varied considerably, with a significant minority of cases being subject to a delay of at least a year. There seemed to be three reasons for such delays.

The first is the sheer volume of business and the limited resources of coroners and their officers. As a result of this some coroners' districts appear to operate with a continuous backlog. One coroner's officer described for us the difficulties which he faced following the Christmas break: "*When we got back we had to administer 120 bodies. This had an inevitable knock-on effect for other inquest preparation because people don't stop dying when there is a holiday.*" We are not well-placed to judge whether this perception of being overloaded is a fair reflection of the burden upon coroner's officers, but this is the sense which they have of their workload, and which they communicated to us.

The second reason for delay is that coroners and their staff may be dependent upon the co-operation of other agencies. Following a road traffic accident death, for example, the coroner is reliant upon the police accident investigator to have examined the vehicles involved, investigated road conditions, interviewed drivers, etc. Similarly, most inquests require reports from a pathologist and, perhaps, a toxicologist. Coroner's officers told us that

---

82 Dorries C., 1999, *Coroners Courts: a guide to law and practice*, Chichester: Wiley, p. 117.
83 *Jervis*, at 169.

much of the delay in scheduling inquests arose from tardiness on the part of other agencies, coupled perhaps with a failure on their part to liaise effectively with the coroner's office.

The third reason for delay is that some inquests are adjourned pending a hearing in another forum – most commonly, a criminal prosecution. We explore this relationship between the inquest and other legal proceedings in Chapter 9.

There does not seem to be any systematic attempt to gauge the impact of delay upon families[84]. This is despite the fact that many coroners have adopted model charters which refer to target times. Typically, coroner's officers bear the brunt of families' concerns regarding delay in the scheduling of the inquest. As one coroner's officer put it to us: "We are the buffer between the police and the coroner, the public and the coroner, and the police and the public". So coroner's officers are well aware that delay is distressing to families, and yet in general they do not appear to think that they can do much to improve the situation.

From the perspective of families, delay in holding the inquest has a number of unfortunate consequences. First, it interrupts the grieving process. Many of those whom we interviewed described the inquest as a hurdle which they had to get over. One informant, who had waited a modest four months for the inquest into the death of his friend, referred to the waiting period as "an eternity". James Fraser, the father of the young boy killed in a collision with a motorcycle (Appendix: Inquest 10), found the six months which he had to wait for the inquest into his son's death an extraordinarily painful time: "Not knowing what's going to happen ... If you're one of those people who wants to get things over and done with, it's no way to go about it. I just feel it's been dragged out unnecessarily."

Apart from being distressing in itself, delay can also affect the quality of evidence given at the inquest. For example, during the inquest into the death of William Bowles (Appendix: Inquest 7), an elderly gentleman killed by a bus, the eleven months' delay between his death and the inquest hearing led to at least two witnesses struggling to recall the details of the accident which they had observed. Similar concerns were raised by Brian Spencer, following the inquest into the death of his sister (Appendix: Inquest 12). As he put it: "Evidence goes stale ... You forget. I was lucky I made notes at the time."

---

84  The Home Office asks coroners to record the time between notification of the death and the inquest. This information is collated and used by the Home Office for management purposes, but not published.

## Liaison between the coroner's office and next-of-kin/potential witnesses

Delay in itself is only part of the problem. It may be exacerbated by what can seem a failure of communication between coroner's officers and the deceased's close relatives. Coroners were keen to emphasise the importance of maintaining good communication with the deceased's family in the period leading up to the inquest, but actual practice seemed highly variable. One coroner's officer described the problem which he faced in trying to reassure a family in circumstances where an inquest was subject to long delay: "*It's distressing because nothing is happening between the death and the inquest. You can't keep ringing up and saying 'Well, we haven't forgotten you' [laughs]. It is very, very difficult because they are just in limbo … waiting and waiting and waiting. After a while they may phone up and I say 'Well, I'm just waiting for this and I'm waiting for that. We haven't forgotten you.'*"

The general impression which we gained was that most coroner's officers were sensitive to the needs of families in this situation and were embarrassed at the delays encountered. They might make several telephone calls in an attempt to reassure next-of-kin that everything possible was being done and that the inquest, when it came, should not be too traumatic. Some of our informants commented favourably upon the care which they had been shown. Others were severely critical, complaining that the coroner's officer who dealt with them had appeared cold or unhelpful. The key issue here, perhaps, is whether coroner's officers regard it as part of their role to offer comfort to families in these circumstances. Some coroner's officers took the view that whilst they should treat families sympathetically, theirs was not a counselling service. Given their workload, they had enough on their plate in conducting a limited enquiry into each death; they had no resources left over which would have enabled them to offer pastoral care to relatives. These coroner's officers would argue that changes in their working conditions, and in particular the increase in their caseload, has led to a shift in focus away from pastoral care of relatives towards a more limited administrative function.

We suspect, however, that this is a matter of personal style, and of the culture within a given coroner's district, at least as much as it is a matter of resources, although inevitably a large caseload means that it is not feasible for coroner's officers to maintain regular contact with families. Coroner's officers pointed to the gradual increase in the number of deaths which they had to deal with (a 20 per cent increase over the past 25 years) which in turn has meant a substantial increase in their workload. Despite this it was our impression that coroner's officers in some districts had an empathetic approach which was appreciated by families. It was also our impression that this caring approach was fostered by individual coroners whose influence percolated down to their officers.

## Anticipating the inquest

Some of our informants were troubled by a realisation following the inquest that they had not known what to expect and, accordingly, that they had been ill-prepared. Many families approach the inquest with questions they hope will be answered, but generally speaking they will not have considered how to go about gaining answers to those questions. They may not appreciate that they can play an active part in the proceedings and, through their own efforts, influence the character of the inquest and what they get out of it. It is only when the inquest is over they may realise that there was this potential and that they failed to take advantage of it. In these circumstances family members could feel very aggrieved that they had not been prepared for the inquest by the coroner and his staff.

Other family members whom we interviewed said that they would have liked to have been consulted on the type of evidence that was gathered and on which witnesses should be called to give evidence. Some coroners appeared to take account of the views of close relatives in this regard, but we do not believe that this was a feature of many inquests. Mr Reynolds, the uncle of two of the four young people killed in a Belgian car crash (Appendix: Inquest 9), was one who felt that there had been a failure of communication prior to the inquest and that this had had a number of unfortunate consequences for the families concerned. In particular, there had been misunderstanding over whether a UK post mortem was required, and secondly, a number of key witnesses were not called to give evidence.

Family members sometimes know what they want to get out of the inquest, but they may or may not be consulted about this by the coroner and his officers. At the very least there needs to be liaison with the next of kin so that their concerns can be made known to the coroner. As it was put to us by Denise and Margaret Hawkes, the sisters of David Hawkes (Appendix: Inquest 14) who had apparently electrocuted himself: "Without information [to begin with] you don't know you can ask for something, or if something is going to be missing." As we have said, this was not a feature of all inquests: there were some in which it appeared that witnesses had indeed been summonsed in response to concerns expressed by members of the family.

It is also important to acknowledge that family members may be in no state to absorb information imparted by the coroner and his staff. Coroner's officers told us that conveying information to the recently bereaved can be extremely difficult. After the shock of witnessing or learning about a sudden death, many people are too confused and traumatised to take in what they are told. Examples were given of relatives who asked the same questions over and over again.

Another problem which can give rise to communication difficulties is that it appears common practice for coroner's officers to liaise with just one person who is taken to represent the family. This may or not be the person who is most affected by the death, and it cannot be assumed in every case that this person will convey information to others who are equally or perhaps even more powerfully affected.

There has been some attempt to improve communication between coroners and families with the introduction of a revised Home Office leaflet *When Sudden Death Occurs*[85]. This leaflet is an attempt to explain the inquest system to bereaved families and witnesses, but most of our informants claimed never to have received it. Some claimed only to have been sent a brief letter advising them of the time, date and venue of the inquest. This was confirmed by some of the coroner's officers whom we interviewed. In some courts the policy was to send the official leaflet through the post; others displayed the leaflet outside the courtroom and simply sent a brief letter to relatives advising them of the date and venue of the inquest.

We were not always convinced that coroners appreciated how limited was the communication with family members initiated by staff in their court. One coroner's officer told us that he routinely advised family members to write down any questions or concerns that they might have and to bring this note with them to the inquest. We observed several inquests in this particular court and there was no sign of family members having heeded this advice. What is more, the coroner seemed disinclined to modify the predetermined pattern of the inquest in response to questions from members of his audience.

The Coroners Officers Association is aware that communication problems can and do arise. Coroner's officers would say that the above-mentioned difficulties have been exacerbated in recent years by the increase in the number of deaths which are handled by each officer, especially in large cities. As a result, many coroner's officers no longer have face-to-face contact with relatives and witnesses. They are effectively desk-bound. In some districts it appears routine for relatives and other witnesses not to have visited the coroner's office until the day of the inquest. This has implications beyond that of the level of support offered to families. In the view of some coroners officers they are now administrators, rather than investigators. Statements from family members may be taken over the telephone, or they may be sent a letter inviting them to prepare a written statement which is then posted to the coroner's office. In other districts the policy would seem to be for a police officer to visit and take a statement. It all adds up to the coroner's officer being an important source of comfort and support to some families, but a shadowy figure to others.

---

85  London: Home Office, 2000. This leaflet replaced *The Work of the Coroner* (London: Home Office, 1996).

In certain types of sudden death (such as road traffic accidents and murders) a police Family Liaison Officer is appointed as the main link with the family. We found that in those cases where the police had assigned a Family Liaison Officer to the bereaved family, the level of concern shown was greatly appreciated. For example, James Fraser, whose son died in a road traffic accident (Appendix: Inquest 10), described how the Family Liaison Officer in his case had visited him and taken him through the evidence which would be presented at the inquest. Mr Fraser had appreciated this visit and the opportunity which it had afforded him to prepare psychologically for the inquest. As a result he was not faced with any surprises and he had a good idea of the scope of the evidence that would be presented. As it happens he had no wish to intervene in order to ask questions – he had, after all, witnessed the death of his son – but it was nonetheless a comfort to know what to expect.

## Conclusion

We conclude this chapter with one question, and one observation. The question concerns the extent to which it is accepted that the inquest is designed to meet the needs of close family and friends of the deceased, as well as to reflect the state's interest in investigating suspicious death. If the inquest is designed simply to give expression to the public interest, including perhaps to highlight defects in services, then on that view there is no need to be unduly concerned with the wishes and feelings of those close to the deceased, although of course one might argue that the wellbeing of those affected should figure prominently in the delivery of any public service. If, on the other hand, we regard the inquest as an occasion when close relatives of the deceased can have their questions answered and their concerns addressed in an attempt to help them to come to terms with the death, this argues for a rather different practice, and one which is more explicitly geared to relatives' interests.

Secondly, an observation: family members appeared more satisfied with the lead-in to the inquest, and with the conduct of the inquest itself, where this was in the hands of a coroner who was prepared to respond to their questions and anxieties. We thought that this attitude was conveyed by coroners to their officers. In contrast, where communication between the coroner and his officers was poor, or where the coroner himself appeared indifferent to the needs of families, families felt short-changed. So each coroner's court had a culture, and that culture was largely determined by the coroner. The courts which were most receptive to the needs of families were those in which the coroner demonstrated through his practice that he was family-orientated, and in which the coroner's relationship with his officers was such that he succeeded in transmitting this value to them.

# Families' experience of the coroners court

There has been no concerted attempt to review the experience of family members who have attended an inquest, although there have been a number of more narrowly focused studies[86]. The bereaved friends and family members who took part in this study had a variety of motives for attending the inquest of the deceased, apart that is from their having perhaps been asked by the coroner's office to give evidence. These included a sense that the inquest provided some kind of closure and a wish to ask questions about the death. Underpinning these various motives was a common view that the inquest experience, from initial preparation to the post-verdict registration of the death, was part of the mourning process. Furthermore, the inquest was perceived, at least in part, as a memorial to the dead person. Consequently, the experience of the inquest had an impact on mourning, and on the way in which family and friends memorialised the deceased. If the inquest was 'good' in terms of matching the families' expectations and needs, this helped the mourning process. If the inquest was unsatisfactory or disappointing, then this marred their memory of the deceased and was an unfitting memorial. For coroners to get the inquest 'right' was therefore very important to those who attended. In practice family members' experience of the inquest varied considerably. In part this reflected their own needs and expectations, but it also reflected coroners' contrasting approaches to the conduct of the inquest.

## Location

Several informants remarked that their first impressions of the location of the coroner's court affected their view of the inquest. Some coroners' courts are situated in rather unsalubrious areas. For example, the route from the railway station to one coroner's court took us through an industrial estate, past a stinking rubbish disposal centre, and through a gloomy damp tunnel paved with bird excrement. This was commented upon by one relative who also took this route. We heard her tell the coroner's officer that she regarded the inquest as an important event, part of her memory of her brother. Having to negotiate bird excreta and the stench of rotting rubbish in order to arrive at the inquest did not make for a fitting memorial.

Other coroners' courts were in similarly rundown areas. This, presumably, tells us something of the status of the coroner's inquiry. Or perhaps it tells us something about the way we regard

---

86  See, for example, Biddle, L. (2002) 'Public hazards or private tragedies? An exploratory study of the effect of coroners' procedures on those bereaved by suicide', *Social Science & Medicine*.

some of the people whose deaths fall to be investigated by the coroner, many of whom have lived life on the margins. One or two courts were new and smart, but it was more common for us to feel that both the geographical location and the decor of the coroner's court reflected a judicial hierarchy in which coroners' courts ranked at or near the bottom.

From the perspective of coroners and their officers the location and condition of the building reflected the resources of the local authority and its willingness to spend money on their service. For many authorities, it would seem, the coroner's court is a relatively low priority.

## Venue

The geography of the building in which some coroners' courts were housed could also appear distinctly unwelcoming. This was particularly true of some older buildings. One coroner's officer commented that the waiting room in his court was so cramped that "it is almost as if the family is an inconvenience. The building fosters that, not us". All too often, therefore, the venue does not help to put families at their ease. This is unsurprising given that most coroners' courts are not situated in a dedicated building, but in, for example, a council office, a police station, or a magistrates' court complex. Some of these buildings had gatekeepers who were responsible for all the various 'customers' entering, and we observed that some of these gatekeepers were ill-informed or dismissive in their response to families seeking directions to the inquest.

In magistrates' courts there was the additional problem that the bereaved family may have had to sit amongst those facing criminal charges. The atmosphere could be loud and rather frenzied. In one case we were fairly sure that a couple arrived for an inquest but were so disturbed by the atmosphere in the waiting area that they left the building.

Coroners' courts that are located in council chambers can appear rather daunting, but there seemed relatively few of those. It was more usual to find coroners' courts situated in refurbished Victorian school buildings.

It is difficult to know how far the character of the venue impacts upon the inquest. For the most part it seemed to us that the character of the inquest was determined by the coroner. But the space in which an inquest takes place must also have some influence, whether in helping the family to feel at ease, or in depressing them by the drabness of the surroundings, or in intimidating them by the splendour of a tiered council chamber.

We also noted that such basic matters as poor acoustics could have a significant impact upon families' experience. In one court the acoustics were so poor that those attending routinely struggled to hear the evidence. One relative, having attended this court, was asked how the inquest experience might have been improved for her. She replied:

> I think meeting, greeting, information before and after, the whole ambience of the place ... a sound system so you can damn well hear.

For all that the venue may be unimpressive, the attitudes of coroners and their officers who work in these buildings can override these unfortunate first impressions. There were some courts where coroner's officers were on the lookout for family members and went out of their way to greet them. In other courts coroner's officers remained hidden away. These differences in the level of care afforded to families attending the inquest were quite striking. It was part of the culture of individual courts, and we suspected that the culture was determined, to a very considerable extent, by the coroner.

## Press attendance

Many of our informants were anxious about the presence of the press in the courtroom. Most coroners with whom we discussed this accepted that the inquest had to be held in public, with press reporting being an inevitable feature of this. Some, however, did contemplate the possibility of selected inquests taking place in chambers. As one coroner put it to us:

> When you have made inquiries and you are satisfied, in the case of a rather tragic suicide, is there any need for the press to be there to pick over the details? There's been enough grief in the family without that. On the other hand, I have to acknowledge that part of the freedom of the society in which we live is because we have a strong and free press.

The attitude of the reporters present can have a bearing on the inquest. We observed some inquests where members of the press arrived in the middle of an inquest and showed scant respect for the feelings of family and/or friends. They were generally young, and sometimes made quite a clatter as they entered. On other occasions we observed reporters chewing gum and reading magazines when the family entered. These attitudes seemed to trivialise the death and showed no respect for the feelings of the family. Coroner A ensured that members of the press waited in a separate area prior to the inquest and made them enter and leave the courtroom separately from the family. Through his firm control over the space taken up by reporters there appeared to be less physical intrusion into families' private space.

## The burden of the inquest

Most of our informants had not had to attend court before. One had attended the inquest of a nephew, another had attended the magistrates' court when her former husband had been charged with violence against her, and another had himself been charged with a minor criminal offence some years previously. But the majority indicated that their expectations of the inquest derived from courtroom dramas on television and in popular fiction. In short, they had very little to go on and were naturally nervous. The difficulty of the occasion could be exacerbated if there were tensions between them and other family members or other witnesses. These tensions were a feature of many of the inquests which we observed.

One manifestation of this lay in the physical positioning of family members and witnesses within the courtroom. We observed several inquests into road traffic deaths where a family member was required to sit very near to the driver of the vehicle that had killed their next-of-kin. One can imagine the feelings of both driver and the bereaved person in these circumstances. In a criminal court, of course, everything is arranged rather differently, although there can be awkward encounters in the waiting area. There was little acknowledgement of the extreme awkwardness felt by some of the participants at the requirement even to be in the same room as someone with whom their relationship was highly charged.

Family splits can also give rise to very uncomfortable feelings and can make those attending very anxious about the seating arrangements in the inquest. We noted instances where estranged family members ended up sitting together, thus adding to the stress of the occasion. In the case of Lee Sharpe (Appendix: Inquest 11), who hanged himself, his partner, Debbie Miller, claimed that Lee's immediate family were hostile towards her following Lee's death. The seating arrangements at the inquest meant that members of Debbie's family were required to sit next to Lee's relatives, despite the bad feeling that existed between the two groups. Debbie had anticipated the inquest with dread, largely because Lee's family had turned against her and excluded her from all their mourning events. Debbie felt that she had been unable to ask the questions that she had wanted to ask at the inquest, for fear of upsetting Lee's family and also because her nervousness and distress had incapacitated her. Observing Debbie in the witness box, we noted that rather than answer the coroner's questions she tended to branch off into statements about her feelings for Lee. It seemed that she was trying to address Lee's family at least as much as she was addressing the coroner and the court.

This was by no means the only inquest which was characterised by feelings of guilt and betrayal. There were several other inquests where family members faced a hostile audience and were apparently intent upon clearing their own name or the name of the deceased. In one extreme example we observed an inquest where the wife of the deceased had been accused of tampering with his oxygen supply. She had to give evidence in front of her accusers. It was, as can be imagined, a fraught and distressing occasion. This was one of several inquests where a member of the deceased's family struggled with feelings of blame or responsibility. In another case a woman was plagued by the thought that she may have been responsible for the death of her mother-in-law in a fire, while another of our informants had been worried about his contribution to the death of his best friend in a road traffic accident. In this latter case the inquest had actually helped this man to deal with those feelings. He felt that both he and the dead man had been cleared of responsibility for the accident.

For those struggling with such feelings the inquest could, therefore, achieve a resolution of sorts. Often, however, that was too much to ask. Whilst interviewing family members we noted that they continued to be burdened by a sense of responsibility for the death. One example was that of James Fraser, who told us that he continued to feel an enormous burden over the death of his son in a road traffic accident (Appendix: Inquest 10). His ex-wife also held him to be responsible, and their relationship had further deteriorated as a result. Mr Fraser appeared a very isolated figure during the inquest. He had wanted to be there, but one did not get a sense that this offered any kind of catharsis:

> For me I suppose the only reason I went there was that I knew I was responsible. So I had to go through the process … the grieving process, healing process, whatever you wish to call it … If that is what it takes to go through these things, then I'll go through it.

But facing a tragedy of this magnitude it would be facile to imagine that the inquest brought an end to Mr Fraser's grieving. As he said to us: "I don't think it will ever stop".

Sometimes we noted a problem of a rather different kind, this being related to the difficulty which some of those attending had with the language and ambience of the courtroom. For example, we observed several inquests where the families' first language was not English. It was apparent to us on several occasions that the family struggled to understand what was being said. We also attended inquests where the family lacked the education, or the assertiveness, to impose themselves on the inquest in order to have their questions answered (or even heard) by the coroner. Accordingly they struggled to understand the inquest or to make an effective contribution to it. Sometimes it seemed to us that coroners or their officers might have made more of an effort to respond to a family who were clearly finding it difficult to understand. As it was, these families were effectively excluded from the inquiry.

## Coroners' management of the inquest

Given that inquests can take place in an atmosphere of fear, guilt, blame and anger, the coroner may be faced with a formidable task if he is both to satisfy the formal purposes of the inquest and go some way towards satisfying the expectations of those present. For example, he may need to identify and respond to tensions among different branches of the family, or between family members and other witnesses. Coroners identified 'loss of control' as one of their principal anxieties. They were constantly aware of the potential for an inquest to fall apart and for emotions to be displayed at their rawest. In general they tried to deal with this by a very careful rehearsal of the purposes of the inquest at the outset.

Some coroners observed that where a case was liable to prove contentious, they benefited from the attendance of legal representatives. As Coroner L put it:

*When lawyers are present it can be more orderly. You haven't got relatives butting in. Because families don't know the rules of evidence … they don't know how courts work. So perhaps someone is in the witness box and I'm taking them through their evidence and they'll say something that someone doesn't like and that person will start asking questions. And you have to say 'Wait your turn!'. By the time their turn comes around they've forgotten the question they wanted to ask in the first place.*

We noted that the coroner's control of the proceedings could be threatened when a family member started to address the court, rather than to ask questions, or where family members contributed from the floor of the court in ways that were unanticipated or unannounced. Coroners differed in the way they responded to these challenges, as they did in the latitude which they were prepared to allow in determining whether somebody was or was not 'a properly interested person'[87]. For the most part coroners did their best to be flexible, responding at least to a limited extent to anxieties expressed by family members. On occasion, however, coroners refused to be deflected, one illustration of this being the inquest into the death of Amanda Barrett (Appendix: Inquest 6). Here the coroner dismissed the questions from Amanda's family concerning her medical treatment, and this failure to engage with the family seemed to us to negate much of the potential value of the inquest.

87  Coroners rule 20, 1984.

After all, there is always the possibility that serious deficiencies have been overlooked in the initial compiling of evidence. What is the point of having a public inquiry into a death if the coroner refuses even to consider questions put to him?

Underlying this case, and others where the failure seemed less stark, is the question of relevance, and secondly, of the scope for family and friends to identify questions that need to be answered and issues that need to be addressed. If families are disempowered from the outset it is very hard for that situation to be rectified at the inquest – although, it has to be said, some coroners did their best to respond to families' concerns at that stage. Sometimes they tried to do this on the day; in other cases, for example the inquest into the death of Edith Spencer (Appendix: Inquest 12), they were prepared to adjourn.

Attributes such as 'warmth' or 'the common touch' are of course largely a matter of personality. It is probably not helpful to comment on this, beyond observing that we were enormously impressed by the common humanity displayed by many of the coroners and coroner's officers whose work we observed. It is, however, perhaps worth distinguishing between two archetypes. Some coroners were not notably empathetic, but they were punctilious and correct in their management of the inquest, and especially in sifting the evidence. They were prepared to engage with the detail of the evidence and to pursue the fullest possible inquiry within what they deemed to be the remit of the inquest. They could also be quite severe in closing off inappropriate questioning or discussion. These coroners did not appear unfeeling, but their attitude to the family was perhaps 'correct' rather than 'warm'. They concentrated upon satisfying the formal purposes of the inquest. Sometimes coroner's officers at these courts made up for the coroner's relative lack of empathy through the consideration which they extended to families. So although we have said that coroners largely determined the culture of their court, it was possible to have a somewhat reserved and 'correct' coroner presiding over a court whose culture, as expressed through the coroner's officers, was warm and empathetic.

The second archetype is that of the coroner who conveys the impression that the inquest is, first and foremost, for the family. These coroners were receptive to family members' uncertain and perhaps clumsy attempts to contribute to the inquest. One coroner told us that he found inquests exhausting and emotionally draining. From the perspective of the family, on the other hand, the flexibility displayed by these coroners was most welcome. They noted the fact that the coroner expressed his condolences with evident sincerity and that he attempted to offer an epitaph for the deceased. Generally speaking the coroner's officers in these courts were viewed in a similarly favourable light. Even informants like Debbie Miller (Appendix: Inquest 11), whose experience of the inquest was very painful, praised the approach of the coroner and his officers. Their careful humanity had made the experience easier for her.

The only real criticism of coroners came when family members felt that they had been treated as if they were of little account. These criticisms arose when the coroner gave the family little or no space for questions, appeared impatient, sped through the evidence, did not offer condolences – or did so in a perfunctory manner, appeared to have more rapport with professional witnesses than with the family, and through his treatment of the evidence appeared to have already made up his mind about the outcome. The following comment, transmitted by e-mail, reflected this view of the coroner:

> My experience was one of individual incompetence, and of poor facilities making it impossible to hear properly. The coroner seemed as if he was reading the report for the first time and wanted to go for lunch. There was no copy of the report presented to us on arrival, which would have been polite. I was also promised that certain medical people would be present to enable us to ask questions about treatment and events leading up to his death, and also to question the post mortem findings.

In our experience it was only a minority of coroners to whom such criticisms could fairly be applied. For the most part families approved the conduct of the inquest. Few could have relished the experience, but the coroner's careful humanity turned a potentially unpleasant event into an experience which had value as far as they were concerned. As a result, the inquest had helped them to come to terms with the person's death.

We cannot expect coroners to be paragons; 'warmth' is not something that can necessarily be learnt. But it is reasonable to expect coroners to be well prepared, and for the inquest to produce a coherent account of the events leading up to the death. In other words, coroners should at least be skilled in marshalling and presenting evidence. Simply through their handling of the occasion they can convey to families that the person's death is being treated seriously. So it is reasonable to expect coroners to be business-like, and not unkind. They should also allow time for questions, and when relatives fail to put these questions in the proper format, they should be patient. They also need at all times to be in control of their own court. Most of the coroners whom we observed achieved this.

# 6                                          Selecting and presenting evidence

According to a recent survey[88], 190,000 deaths, representing a third of all deaths in England and Wales, were reported to the coroner in 1996. The proportion of deaths that are reported has risen substantially in recent years[89]. This of course generates work for the coroner and his officers, and it also represents a much greater degree of intrusion by the state into what would otherwise be treated as a private or 'family' matter. Or to put it another way, it alters the balance between two competing principles – the need for the state to investigate suspicious death and the right of next of kin to privacy and for the rituals of death not to be disrupted. It is argued by some that far too many deaths are now subject to investigation by the coroner service[90]. Our small study threw light on these questions, and in this chapter we reflect on coroners' approach to the selection and presentation of evidence at the inquest. This in turn helps us to establish what the inquest is *for*; and secondly, whether an inquest *need* be held in all the various circumstances in which it is held at present.

Many different kinds of evidence can be required in order for the 'how' question facing the inquest to be answered. Take, for example, the case of David Hawkes (Appendix: Inquest 14). The evidence here was a mixture of psychiatry, forensic science and electrics, not to mention the evidence that David's sisters gave concerning his background and the way his mental health problems had manifested themselves to them. In this case, as indeed in many others we observed, it was not obvious what evidence was relevant to the enquiry. Unsurprisingly, different coroners appeared to adopt different approaches.

If the evidence presented at the inquest is intended simply to assist the coroner (or the jury) to arrive at a verdict, then some medical evidence, in particular, could be dispensed with. Take, for example, the case of James Fraser, the young boy killed in a collision with a motorcycle (Appendix: Inquest 10). Mr Fraser senior queried the need for the post mortem evidence, and given that there was not the slightest doubt that James had been killed in a road traffic accident, he certainly had a point. This was also the view expressed by some police officers who were required to attend an inquest following a road traffic accident death: why could the post mortem not be dealt with by way of a statement? There were several occasions when it seemed to us that the medical evidence could have been truncated – certainly if viewed from the family's perspective, but also from the perspective of the coroner's responsibility to deliver a verdict.

88  Tarling, R. (1998) *Coroner service survey*, London: The Home Office.
89  *Ibid.*
90  Pounder, D. (1999) 'The coroner service: a relic in need of reform', *British Medical Journal*, 318, 1502-3.

Having said this, we observed inquests in which death was apparently the result of a sudden deterioration in a long-established medical condition, or where it was associated with the ingestion of drugs, and in those cases a full rehearsal of the post mortem evidence was justified by the coroner's need to determine the cause of death. In this type of case family members often appeared to be thirsting for information – and were grateful when it was supplied.

Another circumstance in which a careful rehearsal of the medical evidence was clearly justified was that where death was directly associated with some medical procedure. This was the case in Touche[91], and likewise in the inquest into the death of Claire Jenkins (Appendix: Inquest 1). In the Jenkins case, indeed, it seemed to us that the hospital doctor who performed the operation which led directly to Mrs Jenkins' death could have been subjected to somewhat more searching cross-examination by the coroner. For example, was the state of Mrs Jenkins' arteries investigated prior to the operation? Did he accept, with hindsight, that it was a mistake to attempt this operation in her care? Could he be satisfied that Mrs Jenkins' artery did not split because of some mishandling of the tube that was being inserted? Should he, perhaps, have gone more slowly? In fact we had none of this. Clearly, therefore, there is scope for sharply differing interpretations concerning what medical evidence should be presented and, secondly, how searching should be the questions put to medical personnel concerning treatments for which they were responsible.

There is also an issue in these circumstances concerning the ability of a non-medically trained coroner to challenge medical evidence. One lawyer coroner acknowledged to us that he feared he could easily have the wool pulled over his eyes by an apparently confident doctor – especially if that person were a senior figure in the medical world, say a hospital consultant.

An inquest where a medical expert was subjected to quite searching questioning was that into the death of David Hawkes (Appendix: Inquest 14), where David's psychiatrist was required to give detailed evidence of his involvement, and to explain why David was not admitted to mental hospital under section. Some of this questioning was undertaken by the coroner, but much of it was at the hands of David's sisters and their social worker friend. This evidence, it seemed to us, was borderline in terms of its contribution to the coroner's verdict, but it was welcomed by the two Hawkes sisters who had borne the brunt of David's mental health problems over a number of years. Whether the psychiatrist's evidence contributed very much to the question of how David met his death is another question: his evidence was essentially addressing the issue of whether there had been a prior failure of care. It depends, once again, on how broadly one interprets the 'how' question; but as far as the family's needs were concerned the psychiatrist's evidence and the open manner which he delivered it were certainly helpful.

91   R v Inner London Coroner, ex p. Touche [2001] 2 All ER 752.

We found that coroners varied considerably in the patience which they displayed in listening to what could be hours of technical evidence. Take for example the evidence of the accident investigator in the inquest into the death of William Bowles (Appendix: Inquest 7). The coroner's willingness to listen to a wealth of highly technical observations concerning reaction times and stopping distances was impressive in its way – and arguably necessary since he was contemplating a verdict of unlawful killing. In some instances – and perhaps the Hawkes inquest is an example of this – it seemed that the amount of technical material which the coroner allowed to be introduced into evidence reflected what he perceived to be the family's need to have this material put before them. Sometimes we were led to understand that the coroner was aware that the family wished to have medical evidence (for example) fully rehearsed. In other instances this may have been the last thing the family wanted. We suspect that some coroners made an effort to respond to what they took to be the family's views on this question. Others, it seemed, had a more standardised approach – that is to say, they took these decisions without any reference to the family. If the deceased's relatives are reserved, uneducated, or lacking in confidence, they are less likely to make their feelings known to the coroner, and this in turn may mean that they may be denied an opportunity to question a witness whose evidence may have been helpful to them.

## Deciding which witnesses to call

Family wishes apart, we were struck by the extent to which coroners varied in their approach to calling witnesses. Of course it can always be argued that each case is different, and that coroners respond to the particular circumstances, but it was our experience that like cases could be treated very differently, depending on the approach of the individual coroner.

One coroner, sitting in Court 2, explained to us that he believed that all too often the inquest trespassed unnecessarily on private grief. His policy with regard to calling witnesses was consistent with this philosophy since he relied upon written statements to a far greater degree than any other coroner we observed. Medical evidence, for example, was routinely admitted in the form of statements. Sometimes no contentious or difficult issues were raised by the death, in which case this policy seemed perfectly acceptable, and perhaps desirable. In other instances the impression given was that certain matters which might have been the subject of contention, or embarrassment, were brushed aside. One such case concerned a woman who had thrown herself out of a second storey window on the morning she was due to be admitted to a mental health unit of a local hospital. The woman's husband was not asked to give evidence, but he made a number of interventions from the floor of the court.

One of these was to the effect that the medical care of his wife had been inadequate – she had been treated only for a thyroid problem, not for her depression: "*People don't get their act together*", he observed. However, none of the doctors who treated this woman had been asked to attend.

As a result of his general policy of calling few witnesses, inquests in the hands of the above coroner seldom lasted for more than 15 minutes. At Court 10 on the other hand it could seem that every conceivable person who had had some contact with the deceased in the period leading up to his death would be called as a witness – attending police officers, paramedics, and so on, many of whom had nothing to contribute on the question of how the deceased met his death. The contrast with Court 2 was marked. Certainly at Court 10 one had much more of a sense of this being a proper hearing, although the obvious down side was that inquests took a great deal of time and put a number of people to some trouble. At Court 10, if a witness did not turn up the coroner would normally adjourn. At Court 2 on the other hand, if the occasional witness did not appear the coroner would proceed on the basis of statements, as he did for the most part in any event. One particularly striking instance of the greater punctiliousness of the coroners who sat in Court 10 occurred in a case in which some new evidence came to light concerning the deceased's relationship with the owner of an off-licence. This man had written to the coroner, asking to be excused attendance. In the course of the inquest it emerged that he had not been completely frank about his relationship with the deceased (he had been his employer, as well as a friend). The coroner adjourned the inquest in order for this man to be required to attend and give evidence.

The most dramatic illustration of the costs to the family which could flow from a decision not to summon witnesses arose in the inquest upon the two Scott brothers and their friends (Appendix: Inquest 9), held in Court 6. This case demonstrated very clearly the potential clash between what the coroner requires in order to answer the question facing the inquest and the family's need for a complete explanation of why someone they care about has died. Doubtless the presence of the accident investigator and the lorry driver would have made no difference to the verdict in this case, but they might have offered some comfort to the bereaved family. As it was, they were offered only written statements.

This was how one coroner (who does not figure in any of our case studies) viewed the case for calling medical witnesses to the inquest:

> *Certainly, in the tricky hospital deaths, where treatment hasn't quite worked out as everyone had hoped – the relatives think that maybe the doctors are trying to hide something, or the facts haven't come out – if you get all the facts out, so that at least*

*the relatives can say: "Oh, I understand, I see, I'm not entirely happy but at least I now know what happened, thank you very much", that's a very satisfactory outcome. I think the very fact that you are there, impartially, independently, hearing the evidence, dragging the facts out of people, can be helpful to them. They think at least the facts came out and we had a fair hearing.*

One can readily concede the case for not calling witnesses where the cause of death is clear and there is no suspicion on anybody's part of a failure of care, but from the perspective of a bereaved family which is looking to the inquest to provide an account of the circumstances under which a person they cared about has died, to be palmed off with written evidence must be a very frustrating experience.

The family's feelings aside, a lack of evidence may compromise the declared objectives of the inquest. Courts 2 and 5 were most prone to leaving the observer with a sense that there were gaps in the evidence, but at most courts there were occasions when interventions from interested parties suggested lines of inquiry which the coroner might have chosen to pursue but which were destined to remain unexplored because a potential witness had not been invited to give evidence. In the inquest into the death of Claire Jenkins (Appendix: Inquest 1), her friend's interjection, referring to a telephone conversation with a mystery member of the hospital staff, certainly suggested a degree of disquiet on the part of the other staff – whereas the evidence of the surgeon, which was all we had, suggested that everything had proceeded normally. Faced with this new material the coroner had an awkward choice – either to press on regardless or adjourn in order to carry out further investigations. He opted for the former course.

Other inquests gave rise to a similar sense of unease at information being unavailable, although the manifestation of this was usually less dramatic. For example, in the inquest into the death of Gavin Ward (Appendix: Inquest 2) we were provided with a detailed account of Gavin's mental health problems, and of his behaviour leading up to his death. However, one matter which the coroner did not broach at any stage was that of family relationships. It might have been supposed that a young man with this degree of obvious unhappiness would have had some difficulties in his relationship with his parents. In fact the coroner informed us privately that he had evidence which indicated that Gavin had had a very difficult relationship with his mother, and that his father was a short-tempered man who was often violent. None of this figured in the inquest. It can of course be argued that an exploration such as this would not have been appropriate. It would have been intrusive, to say the least. Again, it depends how broadly one interprets the 'how' question.

Some inquests went ahead without evidence which the coroner had clearly wished were available. The inquest into the death of Michael Thwaite (Appendix: Inquest 4) was one example, and in this case the missing evidence would have helped satisfy one of the main purposes of the inquest, namely to establish whether the deceased had died a natural death or had been speeded on his way by a third party. Mr Eliot, who had been in the flat in which Mr Thwaite died, and who had reported his death, did not give evidence. Nor did any of those who witnessed the altercation between Mr Thwaite and another man in the course of which Mr Thwaite was injured, perhaps suffering the haemorrhage from which he died. The lack of evidence in this case may have reflected the fact that Mr Thwaite was a 'down-and-out' who did not merit the concern of the authorities. Had, say, the heir to the throne met his death in this way, one imagines that the police investigation would have been a little more lively. The coroner acknowledged to us privately that the low-key police investigation probably reflected the social status of Mr Thwaite. However, he did not say anything to that effect in the course of the inquest.

Sometimes evidence emerged more or less by chance. Mrs Williams' intervention in the inquest into the death of Claire Jenkins (Appendix: Inquest 1) was one example of this. The fact that this observation was made out of the blue perhaps indicates that friends and family can be unsure as to what matters it is appropriate to put before the coroner. Families told us that they only realised after the inquest was over that they could have asked a question about a certain aspect of the death. Or they realised that they should have alerted the coroner's officer to something that was troubling them. On other occasions we observed family members intervene from the body of the court in order to correct the coroner on minor (sometimes not so minor) matters of fact. Others tried to express more fundamental concerns, but had difficulty wording them appropriately, or in terms that persuaded the coroner that they fell within the remit of the inquest. One can imagine that written statements, upon which the coroner is bound to rely, often fail to reflect all the matters that are troubling the person making them. Sometimes relatives tried to make good these deficiencies in the course of the inquest, but it was difficult for them. This was despite the fact that most coroners were prepared to allow interventions from the floor of the court.

## Is it all predetermined?

What does this highly variable practice in respect of the collection and presentation of evidence tell us about the purposes of the inquest? Perhaps the most obvious observation is that the inquest is not intended to be an occasion when there are any surprises. Often, indeed, the whole thing can seem predetermined. That is to say, the coroner knows exactly what he wants to achieve from the evidence that he has arranged to be presented in his court. The inquest can seem to be a parade of evidence (sometimes, as we have seen, not very much evidence), leading in a direction already determined by the coroner.

So why have an inquest at all when the evidence is clear? The inquest into the deaths of Mr and Mrs Campbell (Appendix: Inquest 3) was a case in point. The police had satisfied themselves that there was no question of foul play. It was not a case where one had murdered the other and then committed suicide: all the evidence pointed to their being a devoted and loving couple. So what was the point of the inquest? The answer, perhaps, is that the inquest ended speculation about the deaths and provided an acceptable account for those who cared about the Campbells and who may well have been disturbed by the manner of their death – especially Mr and Mrs Reed, who had found them. So it is not that the inquest serves no purpose, but it does mean that the inquest is moving on a predetermined course, which marks it out from other courtroom proceedings – both criminal and civil – where the final outcome is in doubt. This can induce a certain cynicism, or weariness, on the part of some of those professionally involved – that is to say coroners and their officers. This is what one coroner's officer had to say on the subject:

> The only time that an inquest serves any useful purpose, I think really, is when people don't know what happened, and they come to the inquest and they listen and they find out what happened. But they are very few and far between. Even in a road traffic accident the police officer will tell them what happened, so we all know what happened. And the other ones are the medical ones – where the doctors have to give evidence and the family get an explanation, if they haven't already had one, as to what happened. But everybody knows that if somebody jumps off a bridge they know what happened, and there is even a video if they want to see the fellow, or if it was a woman, the woman, jumping off the bridge. And they know that what the coroner is going to record is that the fellow killed himself, because that was what he did. I don't see that it serves any useful purpose in most cases because everybody knows what happened. And why have they got to troop down here to the coroner's court? That's what we have got to do, the coroners' rules say that's what we've got to do. And we do.

That is one point of view, although it was not one that was held by most coroner's officers, or indeed by most coroners. But there remains a need to justify holding an inquest, and in some instances it seemed to us that it was quite hard to justify. For example, we observed one inquest into the death of a 91 year old woman, known to have a serious heart condition, who had fallen, banged her head, and sustained a blood clot. She had died in hospital without regaining consciousness. It is fair to say that this old lady's death was not entirely 'natural', but it was still hard to see what purpose was served by having an inquest.

As observers, we often felt that the death was explained perfectly adequately by the coroner's opening remarks, but that did not preclude there being several hours of evidence to follow. Take the case of Gavin Ward (Appendix: Inquest 2), in which there was in fact a day's evidence. The coroner began the inquest by observing that Gavin had been resident in a home which cared for people with depressive illness. He had been found dead on a railway, identifiable only by his fingerprints. He had suffered multiple injuries, consistent with being struck by a train. Although the jury's *verdict* had yet to be reached (and was something of a surprise to us, when it came), in another sense there was little doubt, from these opening remarks, how Gavin had met his death. The inquest was devoted to an exploration of Gavin's state of mind, and the level of institutional care that he had received.

The fundamental answer to this question of why have an inquest at all is, presumably, to set aside any suspicion of foul play. This is true even of the death of a frail 91 year old who has suffered a fall. In that sense inquests are murder inquiries which have been aborted following a preliminary investigation. However, gathering together the various witnesses, and taking their evidence at an inquest, does enable that conclusion (already reached by the investigating authorities) to be examined and perhaps challenged. The inquest is held in public, and the evidence is there to be looked at.

So although the inquest is in one sense predetermined, with all the 'work' having been done beforehand, it is not necessarily a waste of time. Sometimes new evidence does emerge. And then there is the cathartic, or ceremonial, function. But in order for each of these purposes to be fulfilled, one does need evidence. If there are no witnesses there is no chance of learning anything new, and the inquest is also a complete failure as theatre.

Even if the inquest is predetermined, some effort still needs to be put into packaging and presenting the occasion so that it offers a degree of satisfaction to bereaved relatives. In most courts this was done. This led us to view the inquest in the light of a funeral – a kind of state funeral, albeit on a modest scale. In many cases (or, if one agrees with the coroner's officer quoted above, in nearly all cases) the inquest is not truly investigative, but it may still be cathartic to a degree. But where there are no witnesses, the inquest is set irrevocably on a non-investigative course. Not only that, as a funeral, an inquest with no witnesses is a thoroughly inadequate event. At Court 2 we observed inquests where literally no one came. Family members were not called as witnesses, so they chose not to attend. To us, the lone observers, those seemed the saddest occasions of all: state funerals to which nobody came. However, given the inquest's attenuated purposes, and the muted nature of the whole event, one could hardly blame these families for staying away.

# 7                                                  Blame and adversarialism

One of the remarkable things about inquests is that considerable time may be devoted to issues that are explicitly beyond their remit. Another way of putting this is to say that inquests are often dominated by sub-texts, the sub-text being of greater significance to many of the participants than the formally declared purposes of the hearing.

This is recognised by coroners themselves. Coroner H told us that he always bore in mind that the inquest might be the only opportunity for families to have a proper explanation of the death: it was important therefore to explore the circumstances very carefully, even if this was not necessary in order to determine the verdict. Another coroner who had just completed inquests into the deaths of two very young babies commented:

> Two days old I think they both were. Both natural causes, but the parents hadn't understood why their babies had died. And I think this is an opportunity to try to get an explanation so that the parents can have information from the clinicians or the pathologist, and ask questions and can try in some small way to come to terms with their grief. To find out what happened. I think an inquest, if you're doing it well, and you are slightly stretching the rules and going beyond what the statute says, you are providing a means by which people can come to terms with their grief.

Trying to help bereaved people understand the cause of death, in order to help them come to terms with it, is one purpose of the inquest which, whilst not figuring in the rules, is acknowledged by all coroners.

Other sub-texts have to do with the relationship between the inquest and other legal arenas. For example, we observed an inquest into the deaths of two pilots where a key sub-text, understood by the coroner, had to do with family members' intention to claim compensation for their loss. Accordingly, the inquest was focused upon the responsibility of the aircraft company for the crash, with the company (and its lawyers) hoping for an accident verdict whilst the family sought to establish negligence.

## Culpability

This mix of declared and undeclared purposes is one of the keys to understanding the inquest. We found that inquests were often focused upon the one issue which they are quite explicitly not meant to address – which is culpability. Many witnesses and observers were anxious to explore culpability – either to load it onto others, or to deflect it from themselves. There was a time when determining culpability was an explicit and acknowledged purpose of the inquest. Formally speaking, that is no longer the case, but culpability and blame remain as *leitmotifs* which dominate the inquest process, especially in those cases where death occurred following some medical procedure, or as the result of a road traffic accident. This is seldom acknowledged by the coroner, although some coroners had developed a formula for dealing with the issue. For example, at the beginning of any inquest which he deemed 'controversial', Coroner I, having run through the four questions which had to be answered, would announce that the purpose was not to determine any question of civil or criminal liability, or reach any conclusion which pointed the finger of blame … "*However, the facts will be aired*".

Well, what does that mean exactly? How are coroners expected not to point the finger of blame when relatives are convinced that someone (usually an institution) has failed in a duty of care and they are attempting to use the inquest to explore that issue? This is not only a matter of families wishing to extend the inquest remit. There is an inherent contradiction between, say, seeking to establish whether someone died from an industrial disease and refusing to employ the language of blame. If the deceased died as a result of contamination by asbestos, for example, then the inquest is bound to be about blame. The same is true of a road accident death, or a death following a failed medical operation. Coroners become used to wrestling with this conundrum, and some have developed sophisticated formulations which, at least in their own eyes, resolve the issue. For example, one coroner explained his thinking as follows:

> I never start out thinking "Is this going to be negligence?" I start out by thinking "What are the facts?" When the facts come out, it could appear that someone is at fault, or to blame. So be it if those are the facts that come out. I am not allowed to conclude that someone was to blame, but others in court who have heard the evidence can form their own views and go and see their lawyer. But I can only find the facts, and reach the conclusion that on those facts the death was accidental, or misadventure.

That makes sense as far as it goes, but the fundamental paradox of seeking to examine *a death which should not have occurred* without exploring culpability does of course remain.

This was acknowledged by one coroner who complained that the whole system was quite explicitly designed not to achieve what everyone was expecting of it – which was an exploration of culpability. The teeth of the coronial system having been drawn (he said), it was now ill-equipped to deliver that which the general public expects of it. The two key issues in his view were: a) an exploration of culpability; and b) reviewing deficiencies in public services, so defects could be put right. He was uneasy at the development of a blame culture, and felt that the scrutinising of, for example, deficiencies in healthcare could be overdone; nonetheless, this was a legitimate function of the inquest. People wanted to know who was responsible, and they had a right to that information. As for the rest, he saw it as trawling unnecessarily through people's private grief.

It has to be said that an explicit focus upon culpability would give the inquest a coherence that it lacks at present. Most coroners, however, seemed content to proceed on the basis of the inherently question-begging formulations that they had developed. Coroner's officers for their part accepted that families' expectations in this regard had to be firmly reined in. As one explained: "I tell them it's a formality. What you do afterwards as a family is separate." This coroner's officer was troubled by the fact that inquests 'raised expectations', but he had learned to deal with this: "You need to jump on it. If you leave it till the day, the inquest degenerates. The coroner's officer's job is to maintain the dignity of the office of the coroner. It takes a lot of groundwork."

This is a nice illustration of the way practitioners learn to live with paradoxes. Whether we like it or not, some inquests will be about blame. There are many ways in which this can manifest itself. It may not even be about *blaming someone else*. We observed inquests where family members were struggling under the weight of their responsibility for the death of someone they cared about. Mr Fraser (Appendix: Inquest 10) provided one example of this and we observed other, similar cases – such as the man who had driven an overcrowded car containing his children and their friends and momentarily lost control, following which his son was thrown out and killed. In each of these cases the coroner dealt with the bereaved father as gently as he could, but there was no need to tell these men that the inquest was about blame. Mr Fraser, who was a thoughtful man, noted the disjunction between the inquest's limited purposes, as defined, and the rehearsal of so much detailed evidence about the accident:

> It was neither a simple case of finding out a cause of death, nor apportioning blame. They seemed to want to be very careful not to go either way. They said to [*motorcyclist*]: 'In no way are we apportioning blame here' and then they said: 'But what speed were you doing?' And then the barrister got all the photographs on the

*table. Either James was killed by a motorcycle in an accident or he wasn't. The cause of death was that he got hit by a motorcycle. We all knew that. So why go into the rest of the palaver?*

Other inquests revealed a similar gap between expressed purpose and observable reality. For example, the inquest into the death of Gavin Ward (Appendix: Inquest 2) was primarily concerned with exploring the level of care which Gavin had received from psychiatric services and from the staff of the residential unit in which he lived. Mr Ward senior and Gavin's friend, Eleanor Hardy, were given considerable leeway in pursuing *their* agenda, which was to explore the culpability of these services. Mrs Hardy was aware of these tensions. She observed that the limited purposes of the inquest, as explained by the coroner, closed off many lines of enquiry. However, in practice, as she recognised, the question of whether the home had fulfilled its responsibility to Gavin had indeed been explored. She commented that the inquest process was unclear in that it was not explained how far it was appropriate to explore these issues. It was said that they should not be explored, but then the coroner had allowed them to be explored.

Coroners hope that in allowing families to explore culpability, and in facilitating an exchange between professional carers and a bereaved family, they are helping that family come to terms with their loss. If the doctor who performed an operation which went fatally wrong is prepared to turn up at the inquest in order to explain frankly why the person died, that is something that most people will appreciate. Coroners reported, and indeed we observed, that these exchanges could be helpful if the person giving evidence was prepared to address the family's concerns in an open way.

What coroners were concerned to avoid, however, was the kind of aggressive partisanship which is characteristic of criminal trials. Any sign of this made them feel very uneasy. Accordingly they tried to impose some limit upon questioning which was aimed at challenging, say, the quality of medical care. However, there is no clear definition of when this boundary is reached, and no logical basis upon which to determine when it *ought* to be reached. This inevitably gives rise to uncertainty, and to considerable disappointment on the part of some families.

The situation is not helped by the fact that different coroners draw the line in different places. Coroner B in particular could give worried relatives short shrift, the inquest into the death of Amanda Barrett (Appendix: Inquest 6) being one example. The concerns of Amanda's sisters and mother could not be explored at the inquest because of the total absence of relevant witnesses. The coroner was reduced to telling them: *"You'll have to go and see her GP about this … I'm sorry I can't take it any further"*. Mrs Barrett persisted, asking the coroner if he could tell her when exactly Amanda had died. He replied: *"No, I can't!"* When one of Amanda's sisters then said: *"We've quite a few questions we'd like to ask the staff at [hospital]"*, the coroner replied simply: *"Yes, that would be a very sensible idea"* – and left the courtroom.

It is possible of course that the medical care received by Amanda Barrett had been exemplary. But the family thought otherwise and one might argue they had a right to have their concerns addressed at the inquest. If the inquest was not an occasion when the family could do this, then what was it for? Amanda Barrett was, as it happens, a drug addict who had done herself an immense amount of harm – as her family clearly recognised – but there were legitimate questions about the drugs régime upon which she had been placed in the days leading up to her death. The family had arrived at the inquest hoping that it would provide an opportunity to find out exactly what had happened to Amanda. The coroner, because he had not called any medical witnesses, was hopelessly ill-equipped to address their concerns.

Other coroners routinely summoned medical witnesses in these circumstances, in which case there was at least the potential for the family to explore issues surrounding the treatment of the deceased. It was still difficult for families in these circumstances to challenge experts, but some coroners, to their credit as it seemed to us, allowed families considerable leeway and we observed cases in which very searching questions were directed at representatives of medical institutions (or care institutions), many of whom responded with impressive openness and candour.

In the inquest into the death of David Hawkes (Appendix: Inquest 14), the coroner asked David's sisters, on concluding his questioning of David's psychiatrist, whether they had any questions – or whether, perhaps, they would prefer to talk to the psychiatrist privately. As it was, the sisters – and more particularly the social worker friend accompanying them – had some very well thought out questions which they proceeded to put to the psychiatrist over the next 15 minutes. He dealt with these questions reasonably effectively, acknowledging the difficult judgements involved and conceding that she might have been mistaken in David's (non) diagnosis. The result was a very illuminating exchange – more illuminating than the coroner had managed to elicit. In conversation with the coroner's officer after the inquest he suggested that the friend was pursuing her own agenda and had over-stepped the mark. Perhaps that was the coroner's reaction as well, but he did not stop the questioning.

The same coroner, in the inquest into the death of Edith Spencer (Appendix: Inquest 12), agreed, albeit reluctantly, to adjourn the inquest in order to gather more evidence as a result of concerns expressed by the family. He was annoyed that Miss Spencer's niece had not raised these matters earlier, but told us afterwards that he thought he ought to adjourn because the worries expressed were serious and he viewed the purpose of the inquest as being, in part, to satisfy the family.

In most of the inquests in which medical or institutional care was called into question, the exchanges were quite restrained. Witnesses gave every sign of understanding the basis for the family's concerns and the atmosphere was cordial. Occasionally, however, we observed a triumph of adversarialism – seldom instigated by lawyers but generally the result of determined intervention by a member of the deceased's family. A determined parent, such as the father of Andrew Smith (Appendix: Inquest 5), could achieve a much fuller, more detailed inquiry than was the norm. In this case it was far from obvious to the disinterested observer that the mental hospital had done anything wrong. However, the staff's attempt to account for the care provided to Andrew, particularly on the night he absconded, was so full of holes and so implausible in its detail that they made themselves vulnerable. This was the clearest example we observed of the way an inquest can be captured by a determined family member in order to explore issues of responsibility and culpability. Mr Smith was not, as far as we are aware, trained in the black arts of witness interrogation, but some of his cross-examination was quite devastating.

It takes some courage to raise such concerns, and to pursue them. There were other cases where it appeared that family or friends would have liked a fuller rehearsal of these matters, but failed to achieve it. We observed some of these failed attempts, and they had considerable poignancy. Sometimes questions were put to a witness who was clearly not qualified to answer them – as in one case when a pathologist was asked whether a drugs overdose may have been a 'cry for help' rather than reflecting a fixed intention to commit suicide. We observed other interventions of this kind – questions addressed to witnesses who were not qualified to answer them, or speculations which fell some way outside the inquest's remit. Most coroners were patient when confronted with this sort of thing, but it is inevitable that relatives who are told that the issues they wish to raise fall outside the inquest's terms of reference, or that they are beyond the competence of the available witnesses, will feel bewildered and dissatisfied. For the most part coroners were patient, but some could be abrupt, concluding the inquest without ceremony. At Court 2 we observed the coroner leave the court even as questions rained in upon him. In these circumstances the coroner's officer was left attempting to provide some (limited) satisfaction, and there were even occasions when we [researchers] were drawn in, having been identified as professional observers. It was difficult in the circumstances not to take on an advice-giving role, inappropriate as this obviously was.

Education and social class influence the contribution that families can make to an inquest. The Spencer family (Appendix: Inquest 12) were articulate and middle-class: they succeeded in challenging the inquest schedule. Less articulate or less confident families failed to do this: they were unaware of their rights and failed to articulate their doubts. As a result, some genuine and legitimate concerns were not raised, or were raised only in passing. Given that the boundaries of the inquest are so ill-defined, it is inevitable that some families will find it difficult to penetrate the mysteries and thus will fail to influence proceedings.

For the most part coroners were sympathetic and generous in their response to what could be somewhat inchoate anxieties. It was often not easy to see how they were meant to respond. How much ferreting around in the quality of medical care were they supposed to permit? We are not in general critical of coroners' decisions on where to draw the line, or of the manner in which they treated families. But the fact that relatives often left the inquest feeling very disappointed is of course a matter of concern. At the heart of the problem lies uncertainty over the purposes of the inquest, and in particular over the degree to which the 'how' question is meant to be explored. The inquest into the deaths of the four young people in a Belgian road traffic accident (Appendix: Inquest 9) provided the most poignant illustration of this. This family was not necessarily seeking to blame anyone. They wanted information. The moment at the end of the inquest when the coroner prepared to leave and the family sat there in stunned silence was immensely powerful in its symbolism. Here was an occasion which had manifestly and dramatically failed its audience. Admittedly the coroner did his best to retrieve the situation, but given that the family was thirsting for information, the absence of key witnesses meant that the inquest was always going to be a disappointment to them.

This particular inquest presented special problems because the deaths had occurred abroad. Nonetheless we suspect that some coroners would have adopted a much more rigorous approach to the gathering of evidence. They may also have been more attuned to the needs of the family, and would have prepared for the inquest with those needs in mind, fitting the occasion to the circumstances. But whilst some coroners may have anticipated what was required and so responded in a way which meant they more nearly addressed the concerns of the families of these four young people, there is a limit to what could have been achieved under the present inquest format. In part this reflects the limitations of under-resourced coroner's officers, and in part it reflects the limits – the ill-defined limits – upon the inquest's exploration of the 'how' question.

# 8                                                    The verdict

The inquest is an enquiry leading towards a conclusion, that conclusion being encapsulated in the verdict that the coroner delivers at the end of the proceedings. Although coroners are prepared to accommodate a variety of interests and objectives, they have no doubt that their role is judicial, and it follows that one fundamental responsibility is to arrive at a finding of fact. Whether that finding of fact can be satisfactorily encapsulated in the verdict is a moot point: if the purpose of the inquest is to clarify the circumstances leading to death, it is doubtful whether the short form conclusion that is the verdict can adequately describe those events, almost whatever they may be.

All the coroners with whom we discussed this question had a view of their fact-finding responsibilities which went considerably beyond that of arriving at a verdict. For example, Coroner H commented that the inquest was often the only opportunity for families to have a proper explanation of the circumstances of the death. He thought it important to provide this, and therefore to review the events thoroughly.

So on the one hand coroners characterised themselves as judicial officers hearing facts and reaching conclusions, and on the other they saw themselves as having responsibilities *to families* which required them to go some way beyond what was necessary if the objective was solely that of enabling them, as one put it, to *"reach a conclusion"*. In fact the coroner who characterised his responsibilities in this way amplified his statement almost immediately, as follows:

> You've got to try and get the evidence from the witness so that the interested persons will hear the evidence and hopefully understand it. And if you see that they haven't understood it, maybe you'll ask another question that elucidates it a little more for them, or offers them the chance to ask questions.

Some of the uncertainties and contradictions of the inquest are encapsulated in this relationship between evidence and verdict. It was routine for the evidence to be rehearsed in much more detail that was necessary in order to reach a verdict. In large part, it seemed to us, this was for the family. But the fact that some of the evidence may be rehearsed for reasons which have little to do with the straightforward legal imperative of the verdict does give rise to a certain ambiguity within the proceedings. As Coroner C expressed it on one occasion, addressing members of the deceased's family:

*This [the verdict] is not helpful to you, I know, but I hope the exploration of the circumstances has been helpful to you.*

A coroner's officer told us of an inquest where the deceased was an elderly woman who had been in a great deal of pain. She had taken a drugs overdose which had paralysed but not killed her. She had lain on the floor for three days, being eventually found by a neighbour, who also found a suicide note. The lady was admitted to hospital where she apparently expressed regret at her actions. She died there from bronchial pneumonia. At the conclusion of the inquest the coroner had delivered a 'narrative' which attempted to do justice to this complex series of events.

The inquest into the death of David Hawkes (Appendix: Inquest 14) was one where the family (David's two sisters) appeared satisfied both with the verdict and with the coroner's elaboration of the circumstances leading to David's death. What is more, they seemed to see these two elements as separate, but, through the skill of the coroner, as having had a satisfactory relationship forged between them. The inquest had given a helpful picture of David's mental state, validating their experience of him. The open verdict had also seemed appropriate. David may have committed suicide, but equally he may have been experimenting – he was always inventing things. The inquest had acknowledged David's problems, thereby making it understandable why it would not have been appropriate to reach a firm conclusion that he had taken his own life.

That there are these two distinct components to the conclusion of the inquest – the 'story' of the death and the legal conclusion – is supported by our experience of observing Coroner B. As previously noted, this coroner tended to call few witnesses, thus denying himself the raw material upon which to construct a 'story' of the person's death, and he also had an approach to the formal verdict which undermined the obvious dramatic potential of that moment. The verdict was delivered sotto voce and without preamble – very much a case of 'blink and you missed it'. In some instances the coroner had left the courtroom before the family realised that a verdict had been pronounced, and without their knowing what it was. So in the hands of this coroner we had no concluding narrative and a barely audible verdict delivered without ceremony. In the words of one family member:

*I could not believe that was the verdict. He said it, packed up his papers, and walked out. I expected it to be like when you got to a wedding ... when you're going through something formal and you're told what's going to happen and then it happens. I expected him to maybe stand up, tell us he was now going to pronounce the verdict, and then do it, but he muttered under his breath, shuffled his papers, and walked away.*

That was idiosyncratic. It was more usual to observe coroners giving careful emphasis to both elements of the verdict – the story and the legal form.

## Juries

Jury inquests are distinctive in a number of respects, but one of the main differences concerns the prominence given to the verdict. Jurors may occasionally intervene in the course of the inquest in order to question a witness, but essentially their function is to determine the verdict. This alters the complexion of the whole event since the mere fact of this group of people being present throughout the inquest, charged with this one responsibility, means that the verdict is almost bound to assume greater prominence. Our observations inclined us to regard inquests principally as a form of ceremony – a kind of mini state funeral – but the presence of a jury meant there was a much stronger preoccupation with the verdict which they would deliver at the end of the day. This, much more than when the coroner was sitting alone, became the focus of the whole event.

We observed three jury inquests in all. There was one, the inquest into the death of Daniel Evans (Appendix: Inquest 13), where the evidence was limited and the coroner steered the jury towards a 'natural causes' verdict without, it seemed to us, allowing other options to be explored. In fact the coroner suggested to the jury that they might not need to retire in order to consider their verdict. This – the quick canter through the evidence, coupled with the obvious pressure to reach a specific verdict – seemed oddly perfunctory given that a jury had been assembled. If members of the public are to be put to the trouble of sitting on a jury, the least they are entitled to expect is that their task be treated as one of some significance, requiring careful perusal of all the available evidence. In this case the coroner conveyed a sense that the jury's decision was a formality, which is an unfortunate impression to give members of the public performing a civic duty, and one which might also be thought demeaning to the deceased.

But this was not typical, and the inquest into the death of Gavin Ward (Appendix: Inquest 2) provides an alternative model – one in which the evidence was rehearsed at length, essentially, as the coroner explained to us afterwards, because the question of Gavin's intention (whether he had really intended to kill himself) lay at the heart of the decision facing the jury. It is not clear whether the evidence in this case was rehearsed at greater length than usual because of the presence of a jury (this coroner was always most punctilious), but certainly the impression given was that the jury was faced with a decision of some moment which required very careful consideration.

In this case there was no suicide note, and so intention could not be proven beyond reasonable doubt, but the fact of this being a jury inquest meant that the verdict – whether suicide or not – assumed greater prominence than it might have done otherwise. We admired the care shown, and the doggedness with which the coroner pursued that question of intention, but it was nonetheless possible to conclude that the 'narrative' of Gavin's life mattered more than the verdict. After all, how could the jury be satisfied that Gavin had absolutely and unambiguously determined to take his own life? The *story* of Gavin's life, including reference to his many fine qualities, had been very fully rehearsed. That appeared to be of some value to those present. The formal verdict (which, somewhat to our surprise, was 'open') mattered less than the story, but it was given greater prominence than it would otherwise have received because of the jury.

## Suicide

In order for a suicide verdict to be returned, the coroner (or the jury) has to be satisfied 'beyond reasonable doubt' that the deceased intended to kill himself[93]. This is the criminal standard of proof. It is our impression that coroners do indeed set the 'bar' for a suicide verdict at the highest level possible. For example, in the Hawkes case (Appendix: Inquest 14) the coroner decided not to find suicide because of a) a lack of clear evidence of intent – by which he meant that there was no note and the deceased did not make his suicidal intent clear to anyone; and b) he was not sure of the deceased's state of mind at the point when he set up the electrocuting mechanism. The coroner acknowledged in his summing up that the evidence pointed in the direction of suicide, but there was no specific evidence of intent: *"I cannot be certain of his mental condition … the evidence does not fully disclose how it was that the deceased came to kill himself. We know the mechanical means, but not what was in his mind. Was he perhaps experimenting? We cannot be completely satisfied of his intention."* We cannot say that this approach is wrong, but it is certainly cautious. A coroner presumably *could* find suicide in a case such as this, arguing that the deliberateness of the planning demonstrated the requisite intent.

A reluctance to bring in a verdict of suicide was a feature of several other cases we observed, the inquest into the death of Gavin Ward (see above) being one. In that case the fact that Gavin's head had been severed at the neck might itself have been regarded as strongly indicative of suicide, but the coroner did not suggest this to the jury although Gavin's injuries were (briefly) described. As with David Hawkes, there was no unambiguous suicide note and this was deemed sufficient to introduce an element of doubt.

---

93 *Jervis*, 13-22.

We observed another inquest into a death on the railway, held in Court 2, in respect of which the coroner returned a verdict of accidental death. Purely in terms of the verdict, this was the most questionable decision which we observed. In this case much of our information was gleaned from a coroner's officer since, as was standard practice in this court, very little was introduced into evidence. As with Gavin Ward, the neck had been neatly severed, but this was not revealed in the inquest. Furthermore the coroner was aware that the deceased was facing police investigation and was due to be interviewed the following day. Again, there was no reference to this at the inquest. Perhaps the accident verdict in this case was intended as an act of kindness towards the deceased's family (who had been in touch with the coroner), but it certainly brought into question the purpose of the exercise.

Before embarking on this study we would have informally classified as 'suicide' several deaths which, in the event, attracted an open verdict. At the very least we can say that inquest verdicts understate the true level of suicide, even if caution can be justified in the individual case. This is an interesting social phenomenon. It is probably quite widely recognised that a 'not guilty' verdict in a criminal court is not to be equated with innocence, although commentators occasionally adopt the formula that somebody has been 'found innocent'. It is, we surmise, rather less well known that the same reservations need to be entered in respect of the inquest verdict. One coroner told us that one of his officers, in compiling a count of inquest verdicts for administrative purposes, had omitted any reference to 'open' verdicts. When asked why these did not feature, the officer had replied that in his own (private) classification he counted open verdicts as suicides. This was, we believe, a humorous exaggeration. Nonetheless, it has a core of truth.

## Road traffic accidents

One group of inquests that it is implausible to regard as being directed principally towards a verdict are those where death occurred as the result of a road traffic accident. These deaths are all 'accidents' although the degree of culpability will vary. This does not mean that examination of the circumstances is a waste of time, only that it must be intended to fulfil some purpose other than simply to enable the coroner to reach a verdict.

The one exception to this is where the conduct of another driver has been so obviously dangerous, or so grossly negligent, that a verdict of unlawful killing could be justified. This, the coroner made plain, was a live possibility in the inquest into the death of William Bowles (Appendix: Inquest 7). In the end the coroner decided, as he put it, that the evidence in the case 'fell short of that high standard', so an accident verdict was returned.

In most road traffic deaths, however, an unlawful killing verdict is not under consideration, so in that sense the inquest is proceeding along a predetermined path. This does not necessarily mean that the inquest is a waste of time, only that its value has to be assessed by reference to other criteria. The best example of this, once again, was the inquest into the deaths of the four young people in Belgium (Appendix: Inquest 9). This inquest had many deficiencies, certainly if viewed from the perspective of the family, but none of these failures and disappointments had to do with the verdict. The family was concerned that another vehicle may have been involved, but no one suggested that this was anything other than an 'accident', broadly defined. The failure lay in not attempting to give the full story of the young people's deaths, or of their treatment after death. The verdict was an irrelevance.

Coroners and their officers acknowledged that in road traffic deaths the verdict was, in effect, predetermined. One coroner's officer whom we interviewed suggested that there ought to be a special format for these inquests. But it seemed to us that the same argument might be applied to a variety of other specific circumstances. There are so many different kinds of sudden death, with the inquest fulfilling different purposes in respect of each category. What we can say, on the basis of our observations, is that arriving at a correct verdict is only a small part of what goes on in the inquest. If that is the sole or even the principal purpose of the coroner's inquiry, then in most cases the inquest itself could be dispensed with. The coroner already knows the verdict.

This means that the inquest verdict is somewhat of a curiosity. Ostensibly it is what the proceedings are all about, and yet in most cases the verdict could have been predicted from the outset. Despite this, we may have an inquest which is full of passionate argument. The inquest, we would prefer to say, is a story, and every story needs a conclusion. But the verdict is only a tiny part of that conclusion. It is the equivalent, in categorising works of fiction, of labels such as 'romance', 'thriller', 'whodunnit', or 'historical novel'. Simply to apply the label is no substitute for reading the book. Fortunately, most coroners understand this. They allow the story to emerge. Whether we should require all these stories to be told, in a sparsely attended public forum, is of course another question.

# 9                                                    The overlap with other forums

Coroners' powers are now considerably attenuated and an overlap has developed between their responsibilities and the responsibilities exercised in other forums, with the latter, generally speaking, having greater powers. We noted the limitations of the inquest in circumstances where another hearing was anticipated, or had already taken place, in respect of the same event. In principle the overlap may be with a public inquiry (although this was not a feature of our observations), with criminal proceedings, or with a civil action for damages.

Difficulties arising from these various overlaps, coupled with the gradual erosion of coroners' powers, were noted by coroners in their conversations with us, with various possible solutions being advanced. Some of the more thoughtful family members whom we interviewed were also troubled by the overlapping proceedings. For example, Mr Fraser (Appendix: Inquest 10) admitted to being confused by the potential criminal and civil liabilities arising from his son's death, apparently each independent of the coroner's inquiry but nonetheless having some bearing upon it. Mr Fraser had identified this dislocation and was troubled by it; other family members were simply confused.

Coroners often defend their jurisdiction on the basis that it allows them to comment on deficiencies in public services. The relationship between the inquest and the public inquiry (or the putative public inquiry) is, therefore, a matter of concern to them. One problem they identified had to do with the burden of expectation that fell upon the coroner when the family had wanted there to be a public inquiry, had been unable to bring this about and tried to use the coroner's inquest as the best available alternative. Coroners pointed to their limited resources, which meant that they could not possibly conduct the scale of inquiry that a family might be seeking in response to an alleged failure of care (death in prison at the hands of another inmate was one example given). At the same time coroners valued the opportunity, as they saw it, to make general observations which, they hoped, would be picked up by the press. So they did not want to lose any more of their powers – quite the reverse – but they recognised that the various overlapping jurisdictions, operating on different timescales, applying different legal principles, different standards of proof, and with vastly different powers, were confusing to the public whom they were trying to serve. They also could not but be aware that their own jurisdiction was, in terms of the powers which it exercised, very much the poor relation.

There were two main areas of overlap, both of which were prominent in the course of our observations. The first was with criminal proceedings against a person alleged to be responsible for causing the death; and the second lay with the possibility of a civil claim for damages.

## Criminal liability

One of the severest limitations of the inquest emerged in cases where there was alleged criminal liability. The inquest in these cases could be curiously truncated, leading us to question its purpose. For example, what is the function of the inquest when death was the result of a road traffic accident concerning which a driver has already been dealt with on a charge of driving without due care – or, for that matter, is *facing* such a charge? Alternatively, what can the inquest achieve when a parent has suffered the devastating experience of causing the death of his own son in a road traffic accident?

The formal relationship between the inquest and any criminal charge is quite complex. Evidence given at the inquest may be used in criminal proceedings, and the coroner is obliged to warn witnesses of this where it is relevant. The witness does not have to answer questions if the answer might incriminate him. In the inquest into the death of James Fraser (Appendix: Inquest 10), the motorcyclist who collided with James was due to be tried on a charge of driving without due care. He did give evidence at the inquest, albeit briefly. James's father was troubled by the lack of clarity:

> There didn't seem to be much concrete evidence …nothing really solid to back up what people were saying. That was my impression anyway. And because it was just an inquest, it didn't really matter that much. It didn't affect the cause of death, obviously. But either they were trying to find the cause of death, or it was supposed to be a legal case [against the motorcyclist, he meant]. We seemed to be somewhere in between.

In the inquest into the death of William Bowles (Appendix: Inquest 7), in contrast, the bus driver had already been prosecuted and had pleaded guilty to driving without due care. (He had been fined £350 and had eight penalty points imposed.) However, the possibility of a civil action remained and it was this that concerned the driver as the inquest unfolded. A young friend of Mr Bowles who was present attempted to ask the driver about the requirement upon the bus company to limit the number of passengers travelling on the bus at any one time (the bus had been crowded, with several passengers standing, and the driver had said that he was distracted by this.) This question was immediately disqualified by the coroner without explanation. Perhaps he thought it would have some bearing on any negligence action against the bus company. However, this was part of the 'story' of Mr Bowles' death which one might have expected the inquest to explore. Even so, this inquest was much 'fuller' than would have been the case had the charge of driving without due care still been pending. The fact that the criminal charge had been dealt with meant that there could be a full presentation of the evidence at the inquest, including the evidence of the bus driver.

In the inquest into the death of Reginald Hughes (Appendix: Inquest 8) there were two lawyers present, one representing the driver (who again was facing a charge of driving without due care) and one representing Mrs Hughes (who was contemplating a civil action). It seemed to us that the evidence at the inquest was in effect a rehearsal for these two sets of proceedings. The solicitor acting for Mrs Hughes simply took notes, but the solicitor acting for the driver made several interventions, all of them designed to mitigate the more damning aspects of the evidence against his client. The driver, when he was called to give evidence, declined to answer any questions – this on the advice of his solicitor. The members of Mr Hughes' family who were present must have felt frustrated by the driver's refusal to tell his side of the story. The hierarchy was clear: the pending criminal trial took precedence. But it is at least arguable whether the integrity of the criminal trial ought to take precedence over the integrity of the inquest. Finding out how someone died could be deemed as important as deciding whether the driver of the vehicle involved is sufficiently culpable to attract a criminal penalty. As it was we had no evidence from the driver, but protracted cross-examination of the police accident investigator by the driver's solicitor. This, unsurprisingly, drew the coroner's ire: he asked rather impatiently why the solicitor was pursuing this line of questioning when it was obvious to all that the verdict was going to be that of death in a road traffic accident – which, as the coroner put it, "implies no blame against anyone".

It is not only road traffic accidents that may give rise to parallel criminal proceedings. We observed two inquests where the coroner adjourned because there was evidence (albeit tenuous in both cases) that death may have resulted from the intervention of a third party. In each case the police subsequently ruled out foul play. Although nothing came of it in these two instances, it might be argued that these inquests served a useful purpose in that they uncovered evidence (or at least, allegations) which stimulated a police enquiry. In the one case, involving an allegation that a fatal drugs overdose had been administered by a third party, the coroner accepted the need for an adjournment; in the other, where there was an allegation that the wife of the deceased had been complicit in her husband's death, he was initially reluctant, but concluded that he had no option other than to adjourn. (At the resumed inquest the coroner was fiercely critical of those who had made the allegations, making plain his view that they, and the inquest adjournment, had caused the wife unnecessary distress.)

## Civil actions

Equally troubling were those inquests where there were allegations of a failure of institutional care, in which case there was the prospect of a civil action for damages. In these circumstances lawyers were usually present and their interventions, which were designed to protect their client's interest in that prospective civil action, gave a very different feel to the inquest. Coroner H suggested to us that the inquest, as at present constituted, was not an ideal forum for dealing with cases in which there were allegations of medical negligence. He observed that this changed the nature of the inquest, so that it became adversarial rather than inquisitorial, whilst the hospital's legal representation made the proceedings rather lop-sided, with the hospital being determined to protect itself against any verdict that implied a failure of care. This coroner argued that there were other routes which would enable relatives' concerns to be addressed – a complaint to the General Medical Council, or to a medical ombudsman, or else a civil action. It was not the job of the inquest, he contended, to explore relatives' concerns that the life of the deceased might have been saved had there been a better level of medical care. He suggested that this category of case might be removed from the inquest system altogether[94].

Whilst coroners were prepared for, say, a hospital's procedures to be examined, they resisted the kind of full-blown adversarialism that characterises a civil action. In other words they were reluctant to allow the inquest to be used to test the institution's defence to a possible negligence action. That does not mean, of course, that the character of the inquest was not influenced by the prospect of a civil claim[95]. Coroners strove to find a 'middle way' between the nakedly adversarial and the excessively perfunctory. A typical formula, advanced by Coroner I, was that

> where there is evidence of negligence, the inquest can be helpful in establishing the facts …I cannot determine liability, but it is nonetheless my duty to inquire fully and frankly into the facts, and I drag out the facts as best I can. If they have a lawyer present at the inquest then the lawyer will use those facts. If they do not have a lawyer then people can apply for notes of evidence and take them to a lawyer to see if they have a case.

94  Yet another suggested exclusion.
95  And with good reason. See, for example, the award of £500,000 to Christina Steckel, 27, in compensation for the trauma of witnessing her mentally ill brother stab her mother to death and then kill himself. Settlement was against the South London and Maudsley NHS Trust, in whose care the brother was. *The Guardian*, 6 November 2001, p. 8.

Another coroner, Coroner J, argued that in this regard the coroner's inquest was a system in transition. Its basic function, in his view, was to satisfy everyone that this had indeed been a 'natural' death. Failures of medical or other forms of community care should only be explored where it seemed there was a really major problem. Otherwise you were going to have far too many inquests. Also, this could be very unfair on medical personnel – effectively, a civil trial without proper protection for them. Some families, he suggested, wanted to use the inquest as a fishing expedition. One could not possibly hold an inquest in every case in which relatives had concerns.

Other coroners were more accepting of relatives' use of the inquest for these purposes. Coroner I stressed the value of the kind of exchange which *could* take place between a doctor and the family – where, for example, the doctor apologised, and said the hospital had learned a lesson from the death. According to this coroner: *"You can almost see the heat go out of the situation …the family will subside and say something like 'Thank you for being frank, doctor'."* Coroner I thought that hospitals ought to be encouraged to be more open with next of kin, and he regarded the inquest as one means of achieving this because there was, for the most part, a non-adversarial atmosphere and therefore it was one occasion when medical staff could feel safe in making the facts known.

Our observations provided a measure of support for each of these competing views. For example, the inquest into the death of Edith Spencer (Appendix: Inquest 12) was adjourned because the coroner accepted that the concerns expressed by one member of the deceased's family regarding the level of care provided by the nursing home needed to be aired. This, he felt, was not really the purpose of the inquest, but he accepted nonetheless that it was desirable to gather this additional evidence. The family's response at the adjourned inquest suggested that this decision was indeed a wise one.

The inquest into the death of Claire Jenkins (Appendix: Inquest 1) was likewise conducted in a spirit of open enquiry rather than in an adversarial manner and Mrs Jenkins' three friends appeared satisfied with the information provided by the surgeon. It seemed to us that the coroner's questioning might have been more challenging, but whether it would have been appropriate for the coroner to conduct a more searching examination is a moot point. It all depends what one is looking for from the inquest. In the case of Mrs Jenkins the three friends were not inclined to ask questions so it was all left to the coroner. His interrogation consisted of a series of polite enquiries. If we take this to be the model which most coroners would prefer to adopt, one can see that the presence of a determined relative may alter the character of the inquest quite significantly.

The inquest into the death of David Hawkes (Appendix: Inquest 14) provided a kind of mid point between what we have characterised as the polite enquiry and pure adversarialism. The questioning of the psychiatrist by David's two sisters and their social worker friend was persistent and searching, but one did not get the impression that there was any ulterior motive beyond a wish to understand as fully as possible the thinking behind the psychiatrist's decision not to 'section' David. The evidence given in response was in some respects fuller than the coroner had elicited through his own questioning. But the key point, as far as this analysis is concerned, is that all the questioning was geared *to the needs of the inquest* and not aimed at some other forum.

The inquest into the death of Andrew Smith (Appendix: Inquest 5), on the other hand, was adversarial to its core. Mr Smith senior engaged in a protracted cross-examination of the staff of the mental hospital in which his son had been resident, and he in turn had to survive a strong challenge from the solicitor representing the health trust. The circumstances – absconsion from the hospital, followed by drowning (whether deliberate or inadvertent) – were such that it could not have been predicted that a relative, in this case the father, would mount such a determined challenge to the hospital régime. But that is what Mr Smith achieved, and the coroner gave him considerable leeway. The coroner did intervene at one point, observing, perhaps rather plaintively, that the inquest was a limited inquiry and accordingly was not designed to assign blame or attribute responsibility for the death unless the evidence pointed to "*a gross dereliction of a very serious nature*". He said he feared that some of the questioning was straying outside the legal ambit of the proceedings. But Mr Smith was a very determined character, and the coroner more or less gave him his head.

Whilst Mr Smith's cross-examination was effective in demonstrating that the hospital's supervision of Andrew fell below the standard claimed, it does not follow that this kind of cross-examination was appropriate for an inquest. It seemed that Mr Smith was using the inquest as a dry run for a negligence action against the hospital. The evidence that he uncovered in the course of his bruising cross-examination of members of the nursing staff was quite telling, but its purpose lay beyond the inquest. There was no chance of its influencing the coroner's (open) verdict.

What this case demonstrated was that in the hands of an indulgent, or perhaps simply a fair-minded, coroner, the inquest can be captured by a determined family member in order to explore issues of responsibility and blame. If that were the acknowledged purpose of the inquest, one could not possibly object. What is objectionable, perhaps, is to allow the inquest to be employed as a dry run for a civil action. But this is something that the present overlap of jurisdictions, each with their different purposes and interested parties, tends to encourage. What is more, the inquest is on the bottom rung of the jurisdictional pecking order, and may therefore be manipulated to serve ends which are properly pursued in those other forums.

# 10 What is it all for?

The question of what the inquest is meant to achieve lies at the heart of our research. Observing inquests enabled us to compare ostensible purposes with the reality. One cannot judge a social institution by reference to its ostensible purposes – the researcher has to try to deliver a reliable account of what actually goes on. When one examines what goes on within an inquest, it emerges that the practice is highly variable, and often could not have been predicted by reference to the inquest's declared purposes.

The difficulty arises, at least in part, because the inquest has travelled so far from its roots. The original intention was to devise a mechanism to examine suspicious deaths in order to discover whether there had been foul play – in simple terms, to determine whether there had been a murder. One can still see vestiges of this in the modern-day inquest, but responsibility for uncovering a possible murder now lies essentially with the police, and although it is still possible for the coroner to set in train and have some influence upon a police investigation, his role in this respect is now severely attenuated. In the overwhelming majority of inquests there is no suggestion that the death is 'suspicious' – if by that we mean that the deceased may have been murdered. This can contribute to the view, expressed quite forcefully by one of the coroners whom we interviewed, that some inquests involve a quite unnecessary trawl through people's private grief.

Other coroners, whilst maintaining a broadly positive view of their role, acknowledged the problems that arose from the service's layered legislative history and its lack of clear aims. They accepted the need for a wide-ranging government inquiry because they hoped that this would establish what was expected of the coroner service.

The unease acknowledged by some coroners was matched by the puzzlement expressed by some thoughtful family members whom we interviewed. James Fraser's father (Appendix: Inquest 10) was one who identified an incoherence in the inquest's objectives, particularly in terms of apportioning blame as against establishing the cause of death. He said at one point:

> If it is just to find the cause of death, all they needed was, you know, photographs, the situation on the road ... a few basic details. Obviously they will want the post mortem result as well. And that's it. What else do they need if that is all an inquest is for? But maybe that's not all it is for.

Coroners had their own version of what the inquest was for. They had developed their own form of words which they offered to their audience at the start of the inquest. Given that the system they were trying to describe is complex, and lacking any coherent philosophical core, it is doubtful whether these formulations, even when elegantly expressed, contributed much to families' understanding. For example, one deputy coroner's introductory statement included the following:

> *Under the Coroner's Rules I am required to mention Rule 36. The proceedings of the inquest are solely to ascertain who, when, where and how … Neither the coroner nor jury can express an opinion on the 'how'. That is not pertinent to them. We are looking for 'how', not 'why' – that is, we are looking for 'by what means'. The inquest cannot be used to determine civil or criminal liability … I am requested to read this rule out to you.*

In interview with us coroners were concerned to identify benefits that flowed from the inquest. Some placed considerable emphasis upon their power to make recommendations – as in the case, referred to by one, of a badly designed vehicle in which a rear passenger had been killed by an insecure back seat. Following this accident, and the coroner's observations, there had apparently been a redesign. But this sort of thing is so rare, certainly if we can judge by our own observations, that it can hardly stand as a rationale for the whole system. (We also wonder whether there is any system for recording and linking coroners' observations on matters of public safety; if there is not, it does rather bring into question any suggestion that coroners might hope to 'make a difference' in this way.)

One coroner – Coroner H – observed that whilst all inquests had some purposes in common, the inquest could serve many different purposes. This means that each inquest is individual, serving some purposes not served by other inquests. Coroner H suggested, therefore, that whilst there is a core obligation upon the coroner that is common to each inquest, the coroner may be trying to achieve many other things as well – most of them not formally identified as part of the function of the inquest; these additional tasks or aspirations will vary among inquests. We found this analysis convincing, which is to say that it was consistent with our own observations.

## 'How?'

Much of the difficulty in determining what exactly the inquest is designed to achieve can be traced back to the 'how' question. It is the layers of ambiguity surrounding this question, and the many levels upon which it can be answered, which lie behind the elusiveness and complexity of the inquest as a judicial forum. As we have seen, some coroners had developed their own gloss on the 'how' question and might offer this at the start of each inquest. For example, Coroner H had a formula which went something like:

> The inquest is concerned with how the person died, not why. The question of why will be considered only in so far as it helps to determine how.

Unfortunately this does not resolve the fundamental problem. Take a case such as that of Gavin Ward, who was killed by a train (Appendix: Inquest 2). The *how* in this case could be answered quite simply: collision with a train. In fact the inquest attempted to deliver much more than this, especially in regard to Gavin's history of mental health problems, and the level of care offered to him in the home in which he was resident. But we might have had yet more – for example, an examination of Gavin's family history, his relationship with his parents and siblings, and so on. It would all have been relevant at some level. As it was, the inquest focused upon the level of professional care offered to Gavin, but not his family life. That decision can be defended on a number of levels – for example, one might say that to consider Gavin's relationship with his parents would certainly have strayed into *why* rather than *how*. But the same might also be said of the rather searching examination of the level of care and supervision offered by the residential home.

That is not to say that it is not a worthwhile exercise to explore how a person died, only that it is difficult to define the boundaries of that enquiry in such a way as to ensure that the inquest is engaged on a task that is useful and not gratuitous. We liked the following, offered by the coroner at the start of the jury inquest into the death of Daniel Evans (Appendix: Inquest 13):

> The inquest serves a number of purposes. It is to investigate in public things that should be investigated in public. Even if someone dies a natural death in prison the coroner is requested to investigate. There is good reason. Those in prison are dependent on others for their welfare and wellbeing. The inquest is there to remove suspicion and gets to the facts and avoids rumour from ignorance of facts. It is there to give consolation to families.

There are essentially two reasons here, each of which in its own way sounds convincing. It was a shame that the inquest itself failed to live up to this impressive billing.

## Is it for the family?

'To give consolation to families' is not of course one of the formal purposes of the inquest, but it was identified by other coroners likewise (and was clearly visible in the practice of most). The question of how far the inquest is focused on the needs of the family is one which we had in mind throughout our fieldwork. Certainly there were occasions when the inquest appeared to offer some consolation to the family, perhaps because of the coroner's acknowledgment of their loss. In those circumstances it is probably fair to say that the inquest did make a modest contribution to the grieving process. This was greatly facilitated by the natural warmth of some coroners (and some coroner's officers). Words of consolation seemed heartfelt. Some coroners seemed to us to strike exactly the right note, expressing not just a token sympathy but displaying genuine concern for that family and its distinctive preoccupations.

Both our observations and our subsequent interviews with family members confirmed that the inquest can be an event of enormous symbolic significance. It can be a kind of epitaph – a final statement on someone's life and death. Some coroners, it seemed to us, understood this and had a natural warmth and empathy which enabled them to rise to the occasion. Others, rather painfully, did not.

In fairness to those comparatively few coroners whom we might be inclined to criticise for a failure of empathy, they have to respond to a huge *range* of feelings on the part of relatives and witnesses. It is this range of feeling and expectation which in part drives the inquest. Coroners do their best to respond to it. This means that inquests have a highly variable character depending on how those involved feel about the deceased and about the circumstances of his death.

Coroner H was one who confessed to us that he often had no clue how relatives had reacted to the death, or what their needs were. That was something which, generally speaking, only emerged at the inquest. It was very easy in these circumstances for the coroner to 'get it wrong'. We ourselves observed enormous variation in family reactions. At one end of the spectrum there was the sombre, funeral-like atmosphere at the inquest into the death of the four young people killed in the road traffic accident in Belgium (Appendix: Inquest 9); at the other extreme we observed relatives laughing and joking as they entered the courtroom. It is impossible, given this degree of variation in relatives' feelings and in their expectations of the inquest, for it to follow a standard format.

This variation in family expectation, and in the coroner's conduct of the inquest, is difficult to describe and analyse because it applies to two very different dimensions of the inquest, that is to say, its *investigative* function on the one hand and its *ceremonial* function on the other. (By the latter we are referring to the role of the inquest as a kind of public laying to rest – almost, one might say, a state funeral.) Each of these two dimensions may be very powerfully represented; or they may be truncated and barely visible.

There were some inquests which, in our opinion, were rushed and inadequate if judged as a public laying to rest, and which were *also* unsatisfactory if judged by the yardsticks of an investigation. The inquest into the death of Amanda Barrett (Appendix: Inquest 6) was one example of this. The coroner was disinclined to accede to the family's wish to probe further into Amanda's drugs régime, and this meant that there was no meaningful review of the later stages of her life, which meant that the ceremonial component of the inquest was also neglected and inadequate. This reluctance to engage with relatives' concerns was the exception rather than the norm. Compare, for example, the inquest into the death of Beverley Webster (Appendix: Inquest 15) in which the coroner took an enormous amount of trouble to secure a reliable account of the treatment which Beverley had received in her last hours. Unsurprisingly, the family's reaction to this inquest was in stark contrast to that of Amanda Barrett's mother and sisters.

The inquest into the deaths of the Scott brothers and their two friends (Appendix: Inquest 9) might have appeared destined to deliver an anticlimax similar to that suffered by the family of Amanda Barrett, but in the event, even though the investigative component was quite woefully small, the presence of the family in such large numbers, and the eloquent stillness with which they greeted the coroner's attempted winding up of the proceedings, persuaded the coroner in this instance that he had to offer rather more of himself, and also more of the institution which he represented. As the family representative made plain in subsequent conversation with us, most of the family's questions remained unanswered, but they were at least being listened to and this in turn contributed to a feeling that the deaths of these young people were being treated with due seriousness.

This sense of the inquest being an obituary as well as an investigation was a common feature of the inquests we observed, especially in the hands of some coroners. Some witnesses likewise demonstrated through their demeanour, and their comments on the character of the deceased, that they too were aware of the 'funeral' component of the proceedings. Thus coroners and witnesses alike might contribute laudatory observations concerning the deceased's life and character. These comments offered nothing to the investigation, but they were part of the obituary. One example of this arose in the inquest into the death of Gavin Ward (Appendix: Inquest 2), when the coroner spent about an hour questioning Gavin's principal carer in the residential home. Some of this questioning contributed little to answering the questions facing the inquest. But it did provide the audience (including, in this case, the jury) with some insight into Gavin's life and character. The care worker seemed to understand this. For example, at one point he said of Gavin: "*We liked him very much*". There was a similar incident in the course of another inquest when the coroner commented, apropos of nothing at all, that the deceased had had a donor card and that the family had agreed to donate his organs. He made much of the point that this was an unselfish act. Sometimes coroners would bend over backwards to offer an epitaph despite what may have seemed poor material, making observations such as "*I'm sure there was more to* [x] *than we have heard today*". In short, the inquest has the potential, at least in the hands of some coroners, to act as an obituary or epitaph for the dead person. This is not an identified purpose, but it is nonetheless something that many inquests do contribute, and that may be worth preserving.

Another dimension of this question of what the inquest is for concerns the fact that it is, at least in theory, held in public. What is the justification for this? What is the public interest? Should we allow that there is a public interest which overrides what might otherwise have been taken to be a family's right to privacy in respect of painful, personal difficulties? Many families were concerned that the inquest was being reported. Can we justify this public dimension, given that it unquestionably adds to the stress upon some family members?

There is, we recognise, a powerful case for holding inquests in public. It is difficult to see how any suspicion can be removed if the inquest is held behind closed doors. Also, one surely needs an open inquest if public bodies are to be brought to account. At the same time it can feel very uncomfortable to be present when intimate details of the deceased's history and personal relationships are being rehearsed. Certainly the presence of the press on some of these occasions can seem gratuitous. One example concerned the inquest into the deaths of Mr and Mrs Campbell (Appendix: Inquest 3), the old couple who committed suicide together. In this instance there were four young reporters sitting on the press benches, no doubt reflecting the interest which this case aroused in the locality. But was it a matter of legitimate public interest? Perhaps the way in which these old people opted to end their lives when they became very ill and frail is indeed a matter of public interest. But it felt very uncomfortable to be present, and there is certainly an argument for treating this sort of event, once it had been established that the Campbells had not been murdered, as completely private and of no concern of anyone other than the couple's family and close friends.

If, on the other hand, we conclude that inquests have to be held in public, it needs to be said that the inquest as public event has many deficiencies. For the most part, as we observed, inquests are attended only by those who are summoned as witnesses, plus one or two other family and friends, plus a reporter or two. The coroner sometimes appears not to know who is present in court. He may stumble over the identification of family members. The whole thing can seem very low key – which is out of keeping with the personal tragedy which often underlies the proceedings.

Most inquests are not well attended. Typically, there will be a couple of family members, perhaps a friend, maybe a paramedic and a pathologist, plus a reporter. It is a rather sad bit of theatre, with hardly any audience. Perhaps it is no worse than many other courtroom scenes, but a lack of ceremony (and a lack of observers) may not matter very much when someone is being fined for failing to possess a TV licence. It is rather different when one is contemplating the end of someone's life. In the circumstances one can hardly blame family members who are not required as witnesses if they decide not to attend. For those who are left, of course, this only adds to the desolation of the scene.

## Which deaths should we investigate?

The question of what inquests are *for* is closely linked to another, equally fundamental issue, namely, in what circumstances should the coroner investigate and when need an inquest be held? It was put to us by one coroner that many inquests involve excessive interference in the lives of families – all to no good purpose. The question of which deaths need to be investigated through the coronial system is troubling and complex. What is 'sudden' and what is 'suspicious'?

Viewed in isolation, there are many inquests which support the above coroner's contention that the system intrudes unnecessarily upon private grief. Perhaps this in turn reflects the fact that the teeth of the system have progressively been drawn, reaching a point where there can appear to be little left. What *does* remain, on the above coroner's view, is a) an exploration of culpability (albeit this is unacknowledged), and b) scope to explore defects in public services, so these may be put right. This analysis, if accepted – and it does accord with our own observations to a considerable extent – suggests that inquests might be restricted to cases which give rise to suspicion directed at a third party, or where there is a death in prison, plus cases where there is *prima facie* negligence or a failure of care. This would be a more coherent régime, with purposes redefined and capable of being met through the inquest format. The inquest would no longer be concerned with, for example, why people had chosen to kill themselves, or whether someone's suicidal behaviour reflected a fixed intention as opposed to carelessness or experimentation.

This is not a view which we ourselves wish to advance at this stage: we observed several inquests where the deceased appeared to have taken his own life, and in the hands of some coroners these inquests did not seem to us to be a waste of time. Also, if we are to have a more discriminating approach to holding inquests, it is very important that this be based on defensible public interest grounds, rather than – as is certainly possible – an implicit hierarchy of value attached to different people's lives. For example, it would not be acceptable, in our view, were the system to demonstrate a lower level of interest in the deaths of elderly people.

Unfortunately, this issue is more complex than may at first appear. The death of a very old person cannot be said to be unexpected, and many such deaths are, to some degree or other, assisted (whether by the deceased herself, by members of her family, or, as is completely routine, by members of the medical profession). If a 90 year old wishes to take an overdose of tablets, should we regard this as a matter for her, when we would probably not take that attitude in respect of a 30 year old? At what point does a principled wish to preserve autonomy, and dignity, cross over into indifference or callousness?

Part of the problem here may be that the decision whether to refer a death to the coroner will be taken by a medical practitioner, and there is most unlikely to be consistency, let alone a philosophical golden thread, running through all those decisions. It is unlikely, for example, that individual doctors will have a common view as to what constitutes 'suspicion'. One possible way forward, therefore, is to require *all* deaths to be referred to the coroner, removing the present discretion enjoyed by GPs and hospital doctors. That need not mean more inquests. It could well mean fewer inquests, with coroners better placed to forge a clear policy concerning what needs to be investigated by them. It was suggested by one coroner that the doctor's decision whether to refer the case to the coroner was not always taken in the public interest – the doctor might want to conduct a post mortem, but not at the hospital's expense. The doctor may even be intent upon satisfying his own medical curiosity.

If all cases were referred to the coroner (who would presumably have to be assisted by a medically qualified referee) this would not in itself resolve the question of what the inquest is for, or of which cases should be selected for inquest. But it would perhaps provide the basis for a more consistent and coherent policy to emerge.

Essentially the same arguments apply to the post mortem as to the inquest. Again, some coroners suggested to us that post mortems were held unnecessarily. Where the immediate cause of death is known, what is achieved by holding a post mortem? The answer, presumably, is that there is always a possibility that the post mortem and toxicology tests will reveal factors which would otherwise have gone unrecognised, and which in turn might lead the coroner to regard the death as suspicious. In that sense the whole system appears to rest on the single rationale of uncovering suspicion – and, thereafter, of eliminating it. But the inquest as a whole *cannot* be said to be simply about uncovering and removing suspicion. It has many other aspects. The gruesomeness of the post mortem (where it might possibly be avoided) sits unhappily alongside some of these other purposes.

All this suggests that since the inquest has evolved in piecemeal fashion, in response to a host of different influences, there is a strong case for an overarching review in order to bring coherence to a system which now borders on the chaotic, albeit it retains a number of worthwhile features.

# 11          The future of the coroner service

The task of research is to describe and analyse, rather less to make recommendations, and hardly at all to propose new systems and procedures. Accordingly, this chapter will be short.

On one view the whole coronial system is archaic and badly in need of reform. But one has to be careful in reaching that judgement because although a system may be complex and unwieldy, and although it may fulfil purposes other than the acknowledged purposes, it may still be of some use. Furthermore, the purposes that *are* being served may not easily be served in any other way. That, in very broad summary, is our conclusion in respect of the coroner service: the system is incoherent and unconvincing in fulfilling defined objectives, but some good nonetheless emerges from it.

The fact that some relatives find the inquest to be of use in understanding or coming to terms with the death of the deceased, despite the fact that the family's welfare is not one of the inquest's stated aims, points to two possible alterations to the coroner's role. First, it leads us to ask whether the welfare of relatives and other lay witnesses might be made a specific aim of the coroner's investigation and inquest. There are problems with incorporating such an aim, both in terms of drafting and in terms of possible conflict with the interests of witnesses and 'suspects'; the aim could, however, be qualified, being overridden when incompatible with the rights or interests of others. Secondly, our study suggests there is a strong case for greater standardisation of coroners' practice in the interests of family members.

In considering reform it should be borne in mind that, imperfect and variable as the coroner system is in helping relatives to understand the events leading up to the death of a family member, it is, in many cases, the only mechanism which even attempts to do this. There are other forums in which a death may be discussed or investigated, but public inquiries will always be rare, and adversarial trials deal with issues of liability for specific wrongs, in which circumstance burdens of proof and the evidential 'rules of the game' operate to circumscribe the narrative of the death that emerges in court. It is only in the inquest that the deceased is the focus of the proceedings, rather than being a shadowy figure in somebody else's story.

## Different inquests for different circumstances?

We encountered a number of thoughtful and self-critical coroners who were quite prepared to reflect on their role and function. They were not resistant to change as such, merely cautious as to what this change would presage. Others were less willing to contemplate change, and we gained the impression that the coroner service is feeling rather beleaguered, so that any critical comment, even if made with constructive intent, is liable to be perceived as attacking. For the most part, however, it was encouraging to find so many coroners who were prepared to look critically at the coronial system and their own role within it.

One fundamental difficulty that coroners face, and which we have already commented on, is that inquests have to cover a huge variety of circumstances and they also have to satisfy families who have very different needs and expectations. As a result, inquests do not in practice have a consistent format, although there is no formal acknowledgement of this. Should we perhaps consider the case for different levels of investigation, only some of which might involve the public rehearsal of evidence? This issue was raised by one of our informants, the father of James Fraser, the young boy killed in a collision with a motorcycle (Appendix: Inquest 10). He asked us whether it was possible to have *"degrees of inquest"*. This idea of the two-tier inquest (or the three or four tier inquest) masks a number of difficult questions – not least, the problem of deciding which deaths should be assigned to which tier. We suspect that in practice it would be no simple matter to allocate cases in this way. Also, it is not difficult to imagine some families pressing for a 'first-tier' inquest when this was not justified on any objective criteria. Nonetheless, our research does lend some support to the case for a graduated system, if only to bring about greater consistency in the treatment of like cases.

It is inevitable that coroners will have different styles, but the present level of idiosyncrasy goes beyond this, suggesting that there is not always a consensus even with regard to the purposes of the inquest. This is not surprising. There are at least three reasons why coroners act inconsistently, differences of personality aside. The first is that they are trying to pursue objectives (especially in relation to families) which are not formally identified. It is inevitable, given that coroners do *more* than strictly speaking they are required to do, that their practice will vary. The second major difficulty is that inquests cover a hugely variable set of circumstances. Would it perhaps be sensible, as one coroner suggested, to focus on *suspicious* deaths – deaths which may have resulted from foul play – and secondly, deaths in which there appears *prima facie* to be negligence or a failure of care? That might achieve greater coherence. The third difficulty is that coroners have very little power. Their responsibilities are considerably attenuated compared with those of previous generations, so it is to be expected that individual coroners will invent new purposes, as they perceive the need.

## A regional structure?

In addition to a review of the *purposes* of the inquest, there is a case for rethinking the present highly localised appointment system, and building more accountability into it. Should we perhaps have a small number of full-time coroners, each of whom would take responsibility for a *region* and who would act as superintending coroners or as some sort of inspectorate? Reporting to them would be individual coroners, part-time or full-time depending on their jurisdiction or caseload, as at present. This might be a further useful step in promoting a consistent practice (although not as useful as determining what exactly it is that inquests are meant to achieve).

Coroners are of course jealous of their autonomy, but it is necessary to distinguish between *independence* – in the sense, for example, of coroners not being controlled or 'guided' by the authority which appointed them – and *idiosyncrasy* in the sense of individual coroners responding differently to like circumstances. Coronial independence is something to be valued and preserved, and coroners are right to be concerned that their independence may be compromised. There is nothing in our research which challenges the principle that coroners should be free to exercise their judgement, and to do so independently of the local authority which appoints them. But the present multiplicity of local coroners, each autonomous in his or her own court, is a recipe for idiosyncratic practice.

## Coroners and coroner's officers

The relationship between coroners and coroner's officers is another area that might be looked at. As we observed it, this is an arrangement that works extremely well in some courts, less well in others. Given that it tends to be coroner's officers (rather than the coroner) who deal directly with families prior to the inquest, it is important that the coroner and his officers enjoy a good working relationship. The coroner's values and attitudes are transmitted to families through his officers. If the coroner is concerned only with his judicial function, that feeling transmits itself to officers and they themselves are unlikely to develop good working practices or to be sensitive to the burden upon families. If the coroner is family-centred, but has a poor working relationship with his officers, then again families are likely to receive an inferior service.

At some courts coroners and coroner's officers took pride in the fact that they worked closely together (the expression 'one big family' was sometimes used). As we observed them, working relationships in these courts were congenial: each court had a house policy and a house style. A key value was that of support for bereaved families, but another key value was commitment to a thoroughgoing investigation. This was likewise transmitted through the coroner to his officers, although in a way that was perhaps less obvious to us as observers. Equally, there were some centres where it appeared that coroner and coroner's officers did *not* have a particularly good working relationship, where perhaps the coroner's officers regarded the coroner with scepticism for some reason.

Personality difficulties can infect working relationships in all contexts, but the coroner/officer relationship is particularly vulnerable because there appears to be no effective management structure. If the coroner and his officers get on well, that is a matter of good fortune. If they do not get on well, there is little that can be done about it. Coroner's officers are not accountable to the coroner. Their line management is within the police service, and in practice, as several coroner's officers advised us, their police superior is remote and lacking in understanding of the task of coroner's officer or the particular stresses associated with it. In practice, coroner's officers' key working relationship is with the coroner, but in making this relationship work the coroner has to rely on his *personal* attributes; he has no formal authority over these colleagues upon whom he must rely absolutely.

The relationship between coroner's officers and the police service is also in need of reform. It is probably appropriate that coroner's officers be recruited from the police service, but for the police service thereafter to employ and 'manage' coroner's officers is anachronistic. The situation is not helped by the fact that police officers do not hold the coroner's officer role in high regard. Also, the police service is authoritarian and hierarchically driven. The systems of communication that are in place do not encompass coroner's officers. Finding a senior police officer who understands and is interested in the coroner service, and is actually helpful to coroners officers in enabling them to perform their task better, would be a piece of exceptional good fortune. According to the coroners officers whom we interviewed, no one in the police service is concerned with their welfare – for example, the stresses involved in dealing with bereaved families. At the same time coroner's officers tend to claim that no one in the police service could possibly supervise them. As one coroner's officer put it:

> *We are very much on our own, which is strange in this day and age of accountability. We have autonomy – it's the only way it could be done; it's an intense specialisation.*

It follows that training for coroner's officers is 'on the job'. When experienced officers retire, their knowledge goes with them. The remaining coroner's officers will be expected to train any replacement – without, as some were keen to emphasise, any recognition in terms of rank or salary. Despite this sense of being undervalued, coroner's officers, who are overwhelmingly drawn from the ranks of serving police officers, do not favour civilianisation. They have to work alongside police officers, and they tend to believe that an intimate knowledge of the police service is a prerequisite for the job. As one put it:

> They would be fragmenting an already fragmented service. The daily contact [with police officers] would go.

## Accountability and autonomy

It can be seen that accountability and autonomy are continuing preoccupations of both coroners and their officers. Both components of the service tend to see themselves as marginalised and undervalued. Both are convinced of the value of what they do, but believe that this is not recognised by those who are in notional authority over them.

The recent pressure on coroners to prepare model charters suggests that government is aware of the autonomy enjoyed by coroners and is determined to achieve greater accountability and consistency. It seems that the days of the coroner service as a self-governing cadre of specialists may be numbered. We think the proposal for a smaller number of regional coroners, with designated deputies, probably does make sense. So does the proposal to place responsibility for the coroners' jurisdiction at the door of just one government department. But institutional change will not of itself be an adequate response to the present confusions, uncertainties and overlaps that make the coroner service such an intriguing and rewarding subject for investigation. The first task of any review must be to determine what exactly it is that we should expect of coroners and the inquest. From that, everything else follows.

# Appendix: The case studies

In this appendix we provide brief accounts of 15 cases. In each case we observed the inquest, and in seven we also interviewed a member or members of the deceased's family. In some instances we also spoke to the coroner or to a coroner's officer about the case and in those circumstances we make brief reference to those conversations.

We have chosen these 15 cases from the total of 81 inquests that we observed. They were chosen on the basis that they illustrate key themes and issues which struck us in the course of our observations and interviews, and which we elaborate upon in the body of our report.

## Inquest 1
### Claire Jenkins
### Court 9, Coroner C

This inquest was opened six months previously. On that occasion the coroner took evidence from Anne Williams, a friend of Mrs Jenkins. There are three women in the courtroom on this occasion – all in their mid to late 50s and, it may be inferred, friends of the deceased. It transpires that one of them is in fact Anne Williams. There are also two doctors present – one had carried out the unsuccessful operation that led to Mrs Jenkins' death, and the other is the pathologist who conducted the post mortem.

The coroner summarises the earlier evidence. Mrs Jenkins had been a heavy smoker and this had affected her circulation. She had an appointment for an angiogram to be performed. In the course of this procedure the arterial wall split. This problem was at first rectified and Mrs Jenkins was returned to the ward. However, she suffered a cardiac arrest. This was dealt with to the extent that she was able to be placed in an intensive care ward. However, there she died. The post mortem was carried out by a pathologist from a different hospital.

The surgeon gives his evidence. The coroner takes him through his statement. Mrs Jenkins had been referred because she had suffered a blockage of an artery in her pelvis. This was affecting the blood flow to her legs. The careful humanity of the coroner contrasts somewhat with the manner of the surgeon. He appears nervous. Sometimes he laughs inappropriately. The coroner on the other hand is full of solicitude. Occasionally the surgeon counteracts this unfortunate impression slightly in that he directs some of his remarks towards the three friends.

The coroner's questioning is not unduly challenging. He establishes that the doctor has 20 years' experience and that he has conducted this operation on many previous occasions without any difficulty. Mrs Jenkins' case had presented no obvious problematic features. The coroner asks: "Her arteries were fragile?" "Yes." "Would the blockage have affected her life?" "Yes." "Where there has been a leak before, have you been able to recover the process?" "Yes." The surgeon further observes that he has carried out some 2,000 of these procedures over 20 years. Only five resulted in complications, and of these, four were recovered. There was nothing unusual in the technique which he had employed on this occasion.

The coroner asks the three friends if they have any questions – his manner at this point is not encouraging. In fact he says as much – "probably not". The coroner then reads extracts from the report of another doctor. Mrs Jenkins had suffered high blood pressure and a high cholesterol level. The coroner then addresses the three women directly. His manner, as ever, is sympathetic. He observes that this outcome is an uncommon but recognised possible result of angioplasty. It seems that Mrs Jenkins' arteries were in a poor state.

Then we have the evidence of the pathologist. She has been sitting next to the surgeon. The coroner begins by observing: "I don't ask you to read your report – for obvious reasons". He asks her to summarise the factors which contributed to Mrs Jenkins' death. The doctor's evidence, in summary, is that Mrs Jenkins had defective arteries. The stent (device to maintain blood flow) perforated the arterial wall. There is no suggestion that this could have been the result of bad technique.

In the course of this evidence, and somewhat surprisingly, Mrs Williams interjects. She observes that Mrs Jenkins had given up smoking for a year prior to her death. Sadly, it didn't help. It had been explained to her that she had only a 50:50 chance of surviving the operation (this evidence, which is unchallenged, is somewhat in contradiction of that given by the surgeon).

The pathologist resumes her evidence. Basically she attributes death to the state of Mrs Jenkins' arteries, although acknowledging that the immediate cause was the medical intervention. The coroner asks whether there are any questions. Again, his manner is not encouraging. He observes: "I am afraid it is all so clear, isn't it?"

The coroner sums up. He says that he adopts the pathologist's findings as regards the cause of Mrs Jenkins' death. This resulted from a haemorrhage which was in turn due to the perforation of the artery by the stent. Mrs Jenkins had suffered from arterio-sclerosis. The leak was the result of the fragility of her arteries. She returned to the ward where she suffered a cardiac arrest. This had been followed by evidence of bleeding into the stomach. (It had emerged in earlier evidence that it was only Mrs Jenkins' distended stomach that had revealed to the staff of the intensive care ward that she was in fact still bleeding.)

At this point Mrs Williams makes a further interjection. Still seated in the body of the court, she observes that after Mrs Jenkins had been moved to the intensive care ward, she (Mrs Williams) had rung the hospital to enquire about her condition. She had been told over the telephone that Mrs Jenkins *"may be dead tomorrow"*. When asked whether it was possible to see her, this mystery member of the hospital staff had told her that she would rather Mrs Jenkins be left in peace – *"Give her some of the dignity which she hasn't had all day"*.

The coroner shows no sign of wishing to pursue this new line of enquiry. He says that it is something that the hospital doctor will no doubt wish to look into. The surgeon nods vigorously and says that he will indeed do this.

The coroner delivers his verdict – misadventure. Not a death due entirely to natural causes, but arising from a deliberate human act which had taken a turn that led to death. He addresses the three women friends: *"You wanted to know what happened – and I hope you have learned what happened – thank you very much"*. He expresses his condolences. The coroner's officer goes to talk to the three women. The surgeon also waits to talk to them. The coroner's officer ushers everyone downstairs so that they can continue their conversation there. A reporter who has been sitting at the back of the court goes to talk to the three women – and in particular to Mrs Williams. She can be heard saying to him that she doesn't wish to talk any further about the case.

## Inquest 2
### Gavin Ward
### Court 3, Coroner C

This is a jury inquest, and the coroner explains at the outset that whenever there is a death on a railway line the inquest has to be held with a jury. There are nine jury members and each is individually sworn. The language involved – such as 'diligently', 'will a true verdict give', and 'touching the death' – proves difficult for some.

The coroner introduces the case. Gavin's father is present. This same jury has been sitting for two days on another case so the coroner does not have to say very much about the purposes of the inquest. Nonetheless he runs through them.

Gavin Ward had been resident in a private home run by a Fellowship which cares for people with depressive illness. He had been found dead on a railway line just over five months ago, identifiable only by fingerprint evidence. He had suffered multiple injuries, consistent with being struck by a train. The coroner says that he doesn't want to go into the physical details, but Gavin had been decapitated. The investigation had been undertaken by the British Transport Police. Ten witnesses are scheduled, plus three statements. Gavin had left an undated letter addressed to his brother. The coroner says that it is not his practice to read letters, but copies have been made and the jury members will each have one.

The first witness is the project worker who was on duty the night that Gavin disappeared. His manner is calm and he appears not in the least defensive, even though the régime (and his own conduct) are the subject of some criticism from Mr Ward senior and from friends. The project worker's evidence takes about an hour. Much of the questioning contributes little to the issues which are meant to be addressed in the course of the inquest. He says at one point of Gavin: "*We liked him very much*". It was well known in the home that Gavin was potentially suicidal. Various diagnoses had been made of his symptoms – essentially, he was very depressed. It had been suggested that he suffered from Asperger's Syndrome – which includes an inability to understand the subtleties of non-verbal communication. Throughout this interrogation Mr Ward takes notes. The coroner's line of enquiry could be taken to suggest that there was a lack of staff cover in the home. On the night Gavin was found to be missing the project worker was in charge on his own. He had not picked up any indication that Gavin was particularly at risk at that time. This is a gently handled, but nonetheless testing, examination of the procedures in the home.

When the coroner has finished one member of the jury asks a question about Gavin's habit of leaving the home to go for long walks. Mr Ward also asks a number of questions. He appears to be suggesting that there was a lack of alertness on the part of staff which affected the speed of response when Gavin was found to be absent. Mr Ward tends to make speeches rather than to ask questions. This has the effect of getting the project worker to elaborate (in an impressively undefensive way) on his views of Gavin and his state of mind. Eventually the coroner cuts Mr Ward short. He has indeed begun giving his own evidence, rather than asking questions of the project worker.

Then we have the evidence of Mr Ward. He gives the history of his son's mental illness. Gavin had been accepted at university, but had only lasted one term. He had then received counselling from Eleanor Hardy, who was a teacher at his old school. Mr Ward gives the coroner a detailed account of Gavin's mental health problems and of his behaviour leading up to his death. The coroner does not ask about family relationships.

Mr Ward is critical of the home's location near a railway line … *"but you tend to think these experts know what they are about"*. This quotation gives the flavour of the man. He is blunt, perhaps a little abrasive. In all we have a further hour of evidence from Mr Ward. (The coroner later explains to us that he had felt bound to engage in this detailed questioning because there is a lack of evidence regarding Gavin's intention to commit suicide. It is because of the need to be absolutely certain before returning a suicide verdict that he is spending so much time today on the minutiae of Gavin's state of mind and the events of the evening on which he died.)

After a short break we have the evidence of Eleanor Hardy, Gavin's former counsellor. She says that Gavin was always harbouring thoughts of suicide. These thoughts had been a kind of comfort to him – a way out was always available. Eventually they had become friends. She says that she took care to explain to Gavin that that meant that she could no longer be his counsellor. The coroner explores with her Gavin's mental health background. She had thought that he was better – she speculates that it was by virtue of his being better that he had summoned up the courage to commit suicide. She says at one point that Gavin was *"a splendid and remarkable person"*. She says that he was probably wrongly placed at that particular home, although she adds that this was not the fault of the home. However, *"it did seem to me that the systems broke down that night – that more could have been done to find him"*.

Then we have the evidence of the train driver who was the first to spot Gavin's body on the line (not the driver of the train which actually killed him). After the train driver's evidence the coroner is reminded by the coroner's officer that he hadn't given Mr Ward a chance to question Mrs Hardy. Mr Ward does indeed want to do this – so he has another go, mainly offering us his own reflections rather than asking questions.

The next witness is the Railtrack manager who had found the body. The coroner does his best to steer him away from the details of the state of the body: *"Sadly there's no easy way of describing this, but I don't wish you to go into it in any detail"*.

Next we have statements from a consultant psychiatrist who had treated Gavin, plus a statement from Gavin's GP. It is then time for lunch.

We resume with the evidence of the consultant psychiatrist who had responsibility for patients at the home. He had seen Gavin on two occasions, one of them very brief. He described Gavin as suffering from an aesthenic personality disorder. He was shy and withdrawn. He refers to this as a *"persistent style of coping with life"*, rather than an illness. Apparently it is a matter of some academic controversy. The coroner gives Gavin's letter to the psychiatrist for him to read (not aloud). The psychiatrist comments that the note is depressive in character. He says that it indicated that a "*possible future event*" was on Gavin's mind. He says that the letter conveyed a desperately low self-esteem. The coroner refers at one point to "*this question of intention which is so important*".

At various points in the course of this evidence there are also contributions from the careworker and from Mrs Hardy. The psychiatrist observes that people with very low self-esteem find it difficult to cope with adverse life events. Some of us have a pint pot from which we can draw in these circumstances; Gavin had an egg cup. The psychiatrist shakes Mr Ward's hand on the conclusion of his evidence.

Next we have the evidence of another careworker at the home. She is less accepting than the earlier careworker of any criticism directed at the régime. She had "*heard no warning bells*" as far as Gavin was concerned. There is further questioning from Mrs Hardy. She asks the careworker how it had been assumed that Gavin had gone into a local town, given that he had been very sick. Surely that was inconsistent? All the careworker can say is that Gavin had seemed OK to her. The other careworker also contributes occasionally from the floor of the court. Mr Ward also chimes in from time to time. In fact he asks a series of questions of this careworker, most of which she is unable to answer. When she finishes her evidence she asks if she may be released. She leaves the court with slightly high colouring. No glance towards Mrs Hardy or Mr Ward, whose questioning of her has been quite aggressive.

Next we have the evidence of the 'locality manager' for the Fellowship which is responsible for the home in which Gavin lived. This witness explains that it is standard practice to have one full-time member of staff on duty overnight. She observes that the Fellowship felt concern that when Gavin was referred the level of suicide risk was not clearly stated. They were not informed, for example, that he had made a very recent suicide attempt. She observes that the Fellowship has risk management protocols which were adhered to on this occasion. She says at one point: "*If we didn't work with risk, we wouldn't have any clients*". The main thrust of this evidence, therefore, is that you have to care for someone like Gavin somewhere. In fact there isn't the level of care available that someone like him ideally needs. If the Fellowship decides that it can't help him, the only recourse in practice is for him to return to his family. Mr Ward contributes several times from his seat in the centre of the courtroom. He refers to a lack of stimulation for Gavin. However, he also acknowledges that if Gavin felt overstretched he became very anxious. The manager concedes that there may not have been enough going on to interest someone of Gavin's intellectual abilities.

The coroner has taken this evidence with considerable patience. There is, at times, a rather adversarial feel to the proceedings – in particular, Mr Ward and Mrs Hardy appear at odds with the Fellowship. Through all this the coroner allows a considerable leeway to Mr Ward, although he does have a subtle way of closing off discussion when he feels that enough time has been devoted to a particular topic.

Next we have a report from the pathologist. The coroner summarises the statement. Multiple injuries. Decapitated. No blood could be obtained for toxicology. Then we have the next witness, the representative of British Transport Police. The gist of his evidence is that he is satisfied that there were no suspicious circumstances. The coroner asks whether the nature of Gavin's injuries were such as to indicate that he had lain with his head on the line. "Yes", is the answer.

That is the end of the evidence. The coroner sums up. He reminds the jury that the purpose of the inquest is not to determine civil or criminal liability. Nor is it to apportion guilt or blame. It is not open to them to include "those sort of findings" in their conclusions. The coroner reviews the possible verdicts. The first is suicide. This should never be presumed. It must be based on some evidence of intention. That is why he has sought to bring before the jury in such detail what evidence there is relating to Gavin's frame of mind. The coroner emphasises the high burden of proof which must be satisfied before bringing in this verdict. A possible alternative is an accident verdict. The burden of proof here is not nearly so high, but there is no evidence to suggest that this was an accident. The final possibility is an open verdict. This would be appropriate if the evidence does not fully disclose the cause of death. The jury retire.

Whilst they await the verdict, Mr Ward and Mrs Hardy chat together. They tell (researcher) that they don't want an open verdict. That would leave things feeling very unfinished in their view. Mr Ward says that he is satisfied with today's proceedings. However, he says that he would have liked advance warning of the fact that he was entitled to ask questions. He hadn't been prepared for that. This means that he didn't feel that he managed to make the most of the opportunity. But other than that he seems content. Mrs Hardy observes that the limited purpose of the inquest, as explained by the coroner, closes off many lines of enquiry. In fact, she says, there had been issues which had concerned her and Mr Ward, and these had to some degree been explored today. Despite what the coroner had said, there were questions over whether the responsibility of the home had been exercised properly. These had been explored. However, it was not explained how far it was appropriate to explore these issues. It was said that they should not be explored, but then the inquest had allowed them to be explored.

We also speak briefly with the coroner. He says that the main justification for the care, not to say the laboriousness, of today's proceedings lies with the need to satisfy the relatives and other bereaved that the investigation has been conducted properly. It is primarily for them, he thinks.

The jury returns an open verdict.

## Inquest 3
### Malcolm and Paula Campbell
### Court 1, Coroner A

Mr and Mrs Campbell were a couple in their 80s who had apparently decided to commit suicide together when their health was failing. They had died some two months earlier. They had been found by their friends and neighbours – Mr and Mrs Reed – who had had no inkling of what was in their minds. The coroner observes that he had expected a police constable to be present in court to give evidence, but he had not appeared and so he was proposing to read his statement. He would likewise read a statement from the pathologist and another from a friend of the Campbells. The Campbells' GP was present in court and would give evidence, as would Mr Reed. In this instance there was no explanation of the purpose of the inquest, such as appeared standard in the hands of other coroners.

There are four young reporters sitting on the press benches. It would appear that the deaths of Mr and Mrs Campbell have aroused some interest in the local community.

Mr Reed is the first to give evidence. He and his wife had been near neighbours of the Campbells for 25 years: "*We were firm friends*". They had keys to one another's properties. Both Mr and Mrs Campbell were very ill, but when he had last seen them there had been nothing unusual in the way they had spoken to him. Mr Campbell was mobile, Mrs Campbell barely so. Mr Reed had gone round to deliver a birthday cake and through the window had seen two forms on the bed. There was a note pinned in the living room which asked him and his wife not to enter the bedroom. However, he only saw this later. He had gone into the bedroom and had seen the Campbells lying on the bed, each with a plastic bag around their head. There was a letter addressed to him and his wife, and other letters addressed to other friends. The letter to him and his wife had included the sentence: "*We always agreed that when our health failed in old age we would end our lives together*". Mrs Campbell was dependent for her care upon her husband and he had recently had a cancer diagnosis and was not able to contemplate going through with the treatment that was proposed.

The coroner questions Mr Reed with considerable delicacy. At the end of his evidence he thanks him for coming, extending sympathy. He says it must have been a great shock. Mr Reed concurs: "It will be a long time before we get over it, I'm afraid".

The coroner then reads a statement from the pathologist. The post mortem had revealed that both Mr and Mrs Campbell were in poor health. Both were suffering from severe coronary artery disease. The plastic bags were tightly bound around their necks and would have led to asphyxiation.

The coroner reads a statement from a cousin of Mr Campbell. The Campbells had moved to the area 26 years ago. Mrs Campbell's health had deteriorated – she was virtually wheelchair-bound. He was aware that Mr Campbell had had episodes of skin cancer, and recently there had been a further lump found on his neck. It had been proposed that he go to hospital for a daily treatment over a period of six months. The cousin had had a card from the Campbells, saying goodbye. Mr Campbell had said that he did not mean to go through with the treatment. They were "a very loving and devoted couple".

Then we have the evidence of Dr Carlisle, the Campbells' GP. The coroner asks Dr Carlisle simply to read his statement. He does so. He describes various ailments. Mr Campbell now had a further secondary cancer. Radiotherapy would have involved daily visits to the nearest major town for a period of some six weeks. He had not indicated to Mr Campbell that the cancer would be terminal. He had not been given any immediate bad news in that sense. In fact, Dr Carlisle says, he had been reassuring: "There was no reason to suspect that the end was near". Dr Carlisle was aware that Mr Campbell was very distressed at the thought that he would be unable to continue looking after his wife. He did not consider that either Mr or Mrs Campbell was suffering from a depressive illness – in fact they were remarkably cheerful given their various health problems. The coroner sympathises with the doctor: "I am sorry the care you have given them over this period has come to this untimely end".

The police officer not having put in an appearance, the coroner reads his statement. When called by the Reeds, he had found the bodies. There were various stamped addressed envelopes in the house, addressed to various friends and relatives. There were also keys to a number of properties in the area, all to be returned to their owners.

The coroner sums up. Mr and Mrs Campbell were in their 80s. They had formed the intention that once their health deteriorated they would end their lives together. Death would have been quick. This was "a very sad state of affairs", but apparently they had made this decision a long time ago. They ended their lives in a manner which was as peaceful as possible. Verdict: suicide.

## Inquest 4
### Michael Thwaite
### Court 1, Coroner A

Mr Thwaite died five months ago. There is no summary of the facts – we begin immediately with the first witness, who is a police constable. The coroner asks him to read his statement. The officer had been called to a flat in which Mr Thwaite had been found dead. It was a flat rented by a friend of his, in which he had been staying overnight. Mr Thwaite had a history of heart problems. The flat was dirty and damp. Mr Thwaite had blood around his lips. The coroner asks: "*Was there any sign of a struggle?*" None that was apparent.

Then the coroner asks the officer to read the statement of Mr Anthony Eliot, whose flat it was. Apparently Mr Eliot has a vagrant lifestyle. He had not been traced to give evidence at this inquest, although he had given a statement to the police immediately following the discovery of Mr Thwaite. He knew that Mr Thwaite helped out at a day centre. He also knew that he had suffered heart attacks. Mr Thwaite had asked Mr Eliot if he might stay at his flat. He had stayed one week. Whilst there he took tablets and used an inhaler. On the evening that Mr Thwaite had died he had slept on Mr Eliot's floor. When Mr Eliot woke up, he found Mr Thwaite dead.

Then we have a statement from a woman police constable who had been called to a disturbance at the nightshelter where Mr Thwaite occasionally worked. Mr Thwaite had been punched.

Next we have the sworn evidence of a pathologist at the local hospital. He had conducted a post mortem on Mr Thwaite. The immediate cause of death was bleeding in the head. He had suffered a subdural haematoma, leading to swelling of the brain. This was the result of a blow. Mr Thwaite also had a large bruise on one hip, and some other bruises. He also had significant heart disease and very severe lung disease – the airways were blocked, reflecting severe asthma. He also had liver disease and certain other ailments in addition. Despite all the above, the cause of death was the subdural haematoma, itself the result of a blow to the back of the head. The pathologist comments that Mr Thwaite's health was such that he could have collapsed at any time and, as a result of falling, he could have cracked the back of his head. He observes that had he not found the haematoma, his conclusion would have been that Mr Thwaite's heart and lung disease was so severe that it could of itself have been the cause of his death.

Next we have the evidence of Mr Cowan, a social worker who had some responsibility for Mr Thwaite. Mr Cowan confirms that Mr Thwaite drank heavily. He had also told Mr Cowan that he was homosexual.

Next we have the evidence of the detective constable who had investigated Mr Thwaite's death. He had taken statements from residents of the nightshelter. There had been scuffle, but the officer concludes that *"there was no evidence of criminal activity"*. He believes that Mr Thwaite had probably suffered a fall. He doesn't think that there was anything suspicious, either in respect of the nightshelter or with regard to Mr Eliot. Mr Eliot has only a modest criminal record – some petty theft a long time ago. It was not the first time that he had befriended someone and allowed him to stay at his flat – and the other person for whom he had done this recently was still alive. The officer concludes that there were no suspicious circumstances: *"Nothing that raised any alarm bells in my opinion"*.

The coroner sums up. Mr Thwaite had suffered a haematoma which was consistent with either a blow or a fall. An ambulance had been summoned promptly. There had been an incident at the nightshelter. Mr Thwaite had complained that he had been attacked because he was homosexual. The coroner says that he does not consider that the circumstances were suspicious. Nor is he perturbed about the failure to trace Mr Eliot – *"a man of itinerant nature"*. He plays down the possibility that Mr Thwaite may have been struck with a blunt instrument. He says that there is *"no evidence to support that"*. He returns an open verdict.

## Inquest 5
### Andrew Smith
### Court 1, Coroner A

This inquest lasts for four hours. The coroner has warned us that the case is likely to be 'controversial'. Because of other commitments we observe only the first two and a half hours. The courtroom is crowded. There are a number of staff from the psychiatric hospital in which Andrew Smith was resident. Mr Smith senior is also present, accompanied by a McKenzie friend*. There is also a solicitor representing the Health Trust.

The coroner summarises: Andrew Smith's body was recovered from the sea three months ago. The previous day he had absconded from the mental hospital at which he was resident. The coroner explains, with some emphasis, the limited function of the inquest. It is

---

* One who, while not participating in the proceedings, may 'sit, advise and quietly offer help' to a participant.

not a public inquiry. No one can be required to give evidence that may incriminate them. He also runs through the four questions which the inquest is meant to address. He emphasises that the purpose is not to determine civil or criminal liability; however, *"the facts will be aired"*.

At this point Mr Smith queries the non-attendance of the pathologist, the coroner having said that he was simply going to read his statement. Mr Smith says that he had questions that he had wanted to put to him. The coroner asks whether these questions were relevant to the purposes of the inquest. Mr Smith says that they were. The coroner says that if Mr Smith really does want to put questions to the pathologist then the inquest will have to be adjourned. Perhaps fortunately for all concerned, Mr Smith relents and says that he is prepared for the inquest to continue.

The first evidence is from a coroner's officer. He reads the statement of the skipper of the vessel which picked up Andrew Smith's body from the water. Then the coroner's officer gives his own evidence. The main burden of this is that there was no evidence of violence against Mr Smith. Mr Smith had a history of schizophrenia. He had absconded the previous day from the psychiatric hospital. His outer clothing had not been traced. However, his shoes were found a week later near that water's edge. Mr Smith intervenes to make the point that one aspect of his son's illness was that he discarded his shoes.

Then the coroner reads from the pathologist's statement. There were no physical injuries. There was fluid in Andrew Smith's lungs and stomach. No drugs or alcohol. The cause of death was drowning. Next the coroner reads the statement of the project leader of a counselling service to which Andrew had been referred shortly before his death. He had attended a number of sessions. He had expressed hurt and shock at the treatment which he had suffered at the school which he had attended as a boy.

Next we have the evidence of Mr Smith senior. He says that Andrew was a trainee CAB adviser. When aged twelve he'd been sent to private school. Subsequently he had studied at university, but he began to take drugs (around the end of 1997) and this in turn led to behavioural problems. He had left university and his behaviour had further deteriorated. He had been admitted to hospital under Section 3 of the Mental Health Act. Under medication, Andrew's health had improved dramatically. In September 1999 he had returned to university. Andrew had wished to come off the medication he was taking. He had been advised that about a third of those with his condition appeared to recover fully after they had experienced a period of stability. However, Mr Smith says that everyone understood the risk that Andrew would relapse. He completed his degree and trained to be a CAB advisor.

He was very keen on swimming, and also yoga. In April 2001 his behaviour had deteriorated again. As a result, Mr Smith had asked for the community nurse's next visit to Andrew to be brought forward. It was evident that Andrew was once again mentally ill. However, he was opposed to being put on further medication – he was unaware that he was ill and did not think that he needed anything. Mr Smith had urged that Andrew be admitted immediately to hospital under section, but the doctors had preferred to wait until the following day. It was nearly a week later before Andrew was eventually admitted. He was still refusing medication.

Mr Smith had visited the hospital shortly after Andrew's admission and it was decided that Andrew would need medication – this to be forcibly administered if necessary. Mr Smith said that he had stressed to the hospital staff that Andrew needed to be watched constantly. There was no further communication until he was informed that Andrew had absconded. Then he was informed that Andrew had been found dead. Despite his illness, Andrew had given no indication that he was contemplating suicide. Mr Smith said that he found it very hard to believe that Andrew would deliberately drown himself.

The coroner intervenes at this point to say that Mr Smith has provided him, in writing, with "*the bones of a complaint*" against the hospital. Mr Smith says that it is his contention that the hospital was negligent. The main thrust of his complaint appears to be that as a result of the trauma of this further admission under section, and the administration of medicines which were effectively forced upon Andrew, plus subsequent inadequate levels of observation, the hospital had failed his son and contributed directly to his death.

The coroner intervenes to say that he understands that Andrew escaped through a firedoor, following the raising of a fire alarm (which caused the firedoor to be unlocked) – the alarm probably having been set off by Andrew himself. Mr Smith accepts this, but says that in his view the correct level of observation was not exercised. This should have been constant, given that Andrew was known to be at risk of absconding. The coroner points out to Mr Smith that he had earlier said that Andrew was not at risk of suicide (the implication being that, even by Mr Smith's own assessment, Andrew was not perceived to be at risk of serious self-harm). The coroner's approach is patient and painstaking.

As well as being concerned about the level of supervision, Mr Smith contends that Andrew was given inappropriate medication. He refers several times to "*contra-indications*". He says that certain of the drugs administered to Andrew were not appropriate for an agitated or depressed person. So he is concerned as much about the drugs régime upon which Andrew was placed as with the supposed lack of observation at the hospital.

The coroner, whilst polite, is also challenging some of Mr Smith's conclusions. Could the hospital have known that continuous observation was required? Andrew was on a ward which was full of mentally disordered people – was it reasonable to expect one member of staff continuously to look after Andrew?

Before Mr Smith concludes his evidence, the solicitor for the Health Trust puts some questions to him. He asks him whether his various observations are being made with the benefit of any special expertise. What qualifications does Mr Smith have for making these comments about Andrew's drugs régime? This interrogation is quite aggressive – much more aggressive than the approach adopted by the coroner. Mr Smith, however, rises to the challenge. He says that he is not a medical expert, but he knew his son. He had been through his illness with him. He knew his background of running away, and he also knew his response to previous drug cocktails. "My basis for Andrew's needing to be observed", he says, "was my knowledge of Andrew and his illness". Mr Smith repeats that Andrew should just have been given the one drug, rather than the cocktail. Had he been given just the main treatment drug, and not in addition a drug which was designed to calm him down, "he'd still be here now". Mr Smith's evidence has taken the best part of an hour. As he leaves the witness stand, the coroner expresses his sympathy.

Next we have the evidence of a young deputy charge nurse. He it was who had administered the drugs. Andrew had taken these only reluctantly, under pressure from the 'control and restraint' team. He had asked the nurse for appeal forms. Andrew had been placed on 'Level 2' observation – every 30 minutes. The coroner asks whether there were any obvious signs that Andrew wished to escape. No, but it was known that there was an abscondence risk. Mr Smith then puts questions to the nurse. It is not clear what the function of the McKenzie friend is in this instance – Mr Smith seems more than capable of managing on his own. He challenges the charge nurse on the decision to administer the cocktail of drugs. The nurse can only say that these were the drugs that had been prescribed, and he administered them. Mr Smith's questioning is determined and rather repetitive. Eventually the coroner intervenes. He says, albeit in a kindly manner, that the inquest is a limited enquiry. It is not designed to assign blame or indeed responsibility for the death unless the evidence points to a gross dereliction. However, having made his intervention, the coroner allows Mr Smith to continue his questioning. The cross-examination of the charge nurse lasts in all for some 30 minutes. It is not clear where Mr Smith is going with this, since the charge nurse was effectively doing what he had been told to do. Mr Smith is trying to establish a lack of care on the part of the hospital in dealing with his son, but the charge nurse emerges from this reasonably well, albeit he does not give the impression of being very knowledgeable about drugs régimes.

Mr Smith has considerably greater success with the next witness, the nurse who was in charge of the night shift on the occasion of Andrew's escape. In fact, Mr Smith's cross-examination of this witness is quite devastating. Once again the coroner has first go, and asks the nurse to read his statement. Essentially his evidence is to the effect that there was a fire alarm in the middle of the night, following which the residents were woken and assembled as per routine. Andrew was found to be missing. He had not been showing any particular signs of agitation. The coroner asks how many patients were in his care on the ward. Twenty-five. And how many staff were on duty? Three. And of those patients, how many were under continual observation? Two. How many were meant to be under 'Level 2' observation, like Andrew? Four or five.

The coroner stops there, but Mr Smith takes over. He seizes on the apparent inconsistency in this evidence. Effectively one member of staff had 23 patients to look after, including four or five who required observation at least every 30 minutes? Yes. How often had the nurse looked in on Andrew? Twice. Was he doing the half-hourly observations himself? Yes. So in that case why had he only seen Andrew twice? The nurse has some difficulty with this question, as well he might. In fact there is an embarrassed silence. Mr Smith signals incredulity. Then he questions the nurse about his knowledge of the drugs régime. There are a few minutes of this, following which Mr Smith returns to the attack on the question of the impossibility of these three nurses having achieved the level of monitoring that was required in respect of the patients in their care. Another member of the nursing staff who is in court signals to the nurse giving evidence that a documentary record is available. This is produced and it indicates that Andrew was observed by the nurse on several occasions that night – far more than the twice that he had claimed. *"But"*, Mr Smith says to him, *"you say that you only saw Andrew twice"*.

Through all this, the coroner is silently observing. He had previously warned Mr Smith that he was straying beyond the bounds of the enquiry. He doesn't seem inclined to intervene again. The solicitor for the Trust remains silent throughout. The thrust of Mr Smith's questioning is clear: the hospital was negligent in its care of Andrew. Eventually he desists. The solicitor for the Trust asks the nurse if he would look at the record of the observations undertaken by him and by his colleagues that evening. He gets the nurse to confirm that those observations were indeed undertaken.

Mr Smith gets to his feet again. The record indicates half-hourly observations. Was Andrew observed on the half-hour? The nurse concedes that the observations were not always made at the time indicated. Mr Smith asks how it was that three members of staff signed as having carried out those observations – had he not said that the other two members of staff were assigned to full-time observation of two other patients? The answer given is not convincing, and Mr Smith indicates as much with various snorts and gesticulations.

The above is a summary of over two hours of evidence. To the observer it not obvious that the hospital care had been deficient – or at least, that it had been deficient to any major extent. However, the nurses' attempt to account for the care which was provided to Andrew, particularly on the night he absconded, was so full of holes and so implausible in its detail that the impression given was that the hospital was indeed vulnerable.

The inquest lasted a further two hours, in the course of which various other members of the hospital staff, including a consultant psychiatrist, gave evidence. The proceedings were concluded at 6.30 p.m. The coroner returned an open verdict.

## Inquest 6
### Amanda Barrett
### Court 2, Coroner B

Somewhat unfortunately, the coroner begins by mispronouncing Amanda Barrett's surname. He is loudly corrected from the well of the court. Four women are present, and one man. Three of the women are in their late 30s or early 40s and the fourth woman is older. It transpires that the three younger women are Amanda's sisters. The older woman is her mother.

The coroner begins by saying that if anyone wants to ask a question, they should do so. He observes that the inquest was opened by his deputy and that therefore it is necessary for him to go through the identification evidence again. He will read statements from a pathologist and a toxicologist. Ms Barrett had been found to have a heavy drug concentration in her body, but only a modest level of alcohol. At this point one of the women present intervenes. She asks about a letter from Ms Barrett's GP – is it possible to see it? The coroner replies: "Don't worry about that".

The first witness is a coroner's officer. He gives identification evidence. Amanda was a 28 year old shopworker. Her death was the result of chronic heroin abuse which in turn led to pneumonia. The coroner asks whether there is a report from the toxicologist. The coroner's officer replies: "No, I am not aware of one, sir". The coroner sighs heavily. He observes, by way of explanation to the four women, that Amanda had taken a cocktail of drugs and that as a result of that "everything had just shut down".

The coroner's officer is then invited to read the statement of Matthew McGough, Amanda's partner (who is not in court). Amanda had a history of drug abuse, as indeed does he himself. It is noticeable that the sisters shake their heads and mutter as Mr McGough's evidence is read out. However, they do not actually interject. There is similar evidence of dissent when the coroner's officer reaches the point in Mr McGough's statement when he observes that he was not sure whether Amanda was still taking drugs.

The coroner's officer then leaves the stand and the coroner reads the statement of Amanda's GP. Amanda Barrett had presented with abscesses, probably the result of injecting herself with infected needles. She had been injecting heroin for some time. Eventually she had sought help. She was in a bad way – coughing up blood.

At this point there is an interruption from the well of the court. Mrs Barrett (the mother) asks why the GP had given her daughter so many drugs. Amanda had apparently screamed when she was being taken to the ambulance – she feared that she was going to be given yet more drug treatment. The burden of the mother's intervention at this point is that her daughter was being drugged simply to quieten her down. She says rather plaintively: "We need help … we want to get the full picture". She further observes that the nurse had told the family that they were attempting to clear Amanda's lungs of fluid. Did that happen? The burden of Mrs Barrett's remarks is that the family believed that Amanda was not treated properly – that she had been given too many prescribed drugs by her GP and, furthermore, that when admitted to hospital she was not given the necessary treatment to remedy the situation. Her health could have recovered at that point had she been given proper treatment. All this emerges in a series of exchanges between the mother and sisters (seated in the well of the court) and the coroner. None of it is part of the formal evidence of the inquest. The coroner observes at one point: "You will have to go and see the GP about this – it's not how or why the person died, but the circumstances surrounding it".

Although the family gives every appearance of being dissatisfied, the coroner has no more to offer. He says simply: "I am sorry, I can't take it any further". He starts to deliver his verdict, but again one of the sisters interrupts. But the coroner's patience is exhausted. He continues with his peroration. This was an accidental death. Mrs Barrett asks him: "Can you tell me the time she died?" "No", the coroner replies shortly, "I can't". One of Amanda's sisters says to him: "We've got quite a few questions we'd like to ask the staff at the hospital." "Yes", says the coroner, "that would be a very sensible idea". He gets up and walks out.

After the inquest we speak to Amanda's mother and sisters. They are extremely upset. They had been expecting far more from the inquest. They wonder what they can do now to get to the bottom of Amanda's death.

**Inquest 7**
**William Bowles**
**Court 10, Coroner H**

This is the inquest into the death of William Bowles, who died from injuries sustained in a road traffic accident eleven months ago. Mr Bowles was knocked over by a bus.

The bus driver is present in court and he has a solicitor in attendance. It emerges in the course of the inquest that the driver has been prosecuted and that he pleaded guilty to driving without due care and attention. He was fined £350 and had eight penalty points imposed. There are also various friends or family of the bus driver present, and they are sitting in the row in front of the friends and family of Mr Bowles. There is, in other words, an awkward proximity.

The inquest begins with the coroners officer announcing the first witness, but the coroner interrupts to explain the history of the adjourned inquest. He expresses sympathy to the family of Mr Bowles, and then provides an explanation of the nature and scope of the inquest.

The first witness is Joanne Moody, who is a relative of Mr Bowles. She is a young woman of about 20 or so. She had last seen Mr Bowles a week before his death. He walked with a stick, and was occasionally unsteady. He had had one recent fall but was generally OK. He had had cataracts but his eyesight had been reasonable. His hearing was also adequate as far as she knew. He had been physically and mentally well when she last saw him. He regularly crossed the road at the point where the accident happened. The coroner elicits this information in a low-key manner and asks the witness if there is anything she feels she hasn't covered. No. Does the solicitor for the driver have any questions? No.

Next we have the evidence of the accident investigator, an experienced police constable. He provides a fairly speedy run-through of the road conditions. There was a compulsory bus stop just before the point at which Mr Bowles was killed. He has photographs of the scene. The investigator stands down, but is to be re-called later.

The next witness is a young woman who was on the bus and had seen the accident. She thought the bus was travelling quickly, but not outrageously so. She had seen Mr Bowles crossing the road ahead. He had passed the traffic island in the middle of the road and was on their side of the road. He was walking slowly, bent over and looking at the ground, not towards the bus. The bus had taken no avoiding action until the last minute when the driver had obviously seen the man and tried to swerve. There had been no reduction in speed prior to that. The coroner leads the witness through her statement. The picture which emerges is of the driver having unaccountably failed to see this old man crossing the road in front of him.

Then we have another witness – a young Yugoslav. He was also on the bus, and once again the coroner leads him through his statement. Some discrepancies emerge between his oral evidence and his written statement, but nothing of great significance. This witness had seen the man walk the entire width of the road, including passing the traffic island in the middle. Once again there are no questions, although the bus driver is evidently concerned and asks for a quick word with his solicitor. The coroner allows this, but following the 'word' there are still no questions.

The third witness is a young woman who was waiting at the bus stop. She was concerned at the time that the bus was going to carry on without stopping. It did not reduce speed or deviate. It was going at a normal speed for the road. Again the coroner is concerned that at certain points the witness appears to be departing from her written statement. She points out that nearly a year has passed since she made it. Again there are no questions.

Next we have the evidence of the police officer who first arrived at the scene. He breath-tested the driver (negative) and also took a statement from him on the spot. The driver had told the officer that he had not seen the pedestrian until the last moment. Then we have a medical report read to the court. Mr Bowles's injuries were consistent with his having been struck by a moving vehicle.

Next we have the oral evidence of the pathologist. Mr Bowles had suffered a severe skull fracture and injuries to the brain.

Next the accident investigator is re-called. This inquest is moving at an extremely slow pace. The coroner establishes that there were no defects with the bus. The accident investigator estimates that it would have taken Mr Bowles nine seconds to cross the road. The bus driver had him in vision for nearly a hundred metres. The speed of impact is estimated at 20-25 miles an hour – the bus had managed to stop within its own length. The accident investigator gives it as his opinion that the driver had failed to maintain a proper observation. Had he looked ahead, and slowed when he first saw Mr Bowles, he probably would not even have had to stop. The coroner again invites questions and none is forthcoming. The driver is again concerned and asks to speak to his solicitor. This time hey actually leave the courtroom. There is a delay of a few minutes or so, following which there are again no questions.

The coroner then refers to criminal proceedings having taken place. At this point the solicitor for the bus driver stands up to say that he objects to there being any account of those proceedings at this inquest. The coroner rather brushes this aside – he says he has no intention of doing that.

The final witness is the bus driver. The coroner explains to him that he doesn't have to answer questions which expose him to criminal liability or to a civil action. The gist of the driver's evidence is that he was preoccupied with the number of people on his bus (it was very crowded) and was checking whether any of them might want to stop at the bus stop which he was approaching. He then became conscious of people at the bus stop becoming agitated – waving – when it became clear to them that he was not proposing to stop. So he was distracted by that and only saw Mr Bowles at the last moment.

Ms Moody says she wants to ask a question. She asks about the requirement upon the bus company to limit the number of passengers travelling on the bus at any one time. The coroner speedily disallows this question. This is on the face of it surprising because the question bears on the driver's evidence that he had been distracted by the number of passengers on board and that he was concerned for the safety of his standing passengers in particular, thus affecting his braking. At this point the solicitor for the bus driver asks his client just one question – why did he not stop at the bus stop. The answer is that he'd ascertained that none of his own passengers wished to alight and that there was no room to take anyone else on.

Then we have the coroner's summing up of the evidence. The cause of death is clear – Mr Bowles had suffered multiple injuries. He says that he hopes it will be of some comfort to the family that Mr Bowles would have had little or no awareness of the severity of those injuries. He makes a number of quite damning comments about the conduct of the driver. He makes it plain that the bus could have stopped completely, or substantially slowed down, given the time which Mr Bowles had been in view. He says: "*This collision was avoidable*". The coroner makes these points with considerable force.

Then the coroner comes to the verdict. He explains that it is only where conduct has been grossly negligent, or where driving has been obviously dangerous, that a verdict of unlawful killing is justified. He says that the evidence in this case falls short of that high standard. He says that a verdict of accidental death is appropriate even where there is, as in this case, a measure of culpability. So that is the verdict. The coroner thanks the witnesses. He extends his deepest sympathy to those who were close to Mr Bowles.

## Inquest 8
**Reginald Hughes**
**Court 6, Coroner F**

This is one of three inquests scheduled for this afternoon – all road traffic accidents. The courtroom is rather imposing, with tiered leather-clad seating. There is a round table in the well of the court and room for some 80 people in the whole amphitheatre. The driver of the car that killed Mr Hughes is present, accompanied by a solicitor. Before the inquest starts the solicitor checks whether there is to be a criminal prosecution. He is informed that summonses are being prepared. For what? he asks. Careless driving. So not Section 1 (dangerous driving)? The police sergeant replies: "*Oh good God, no. This was never a Section 1 accident.*" Various people gather and sit dotted around the courtroom. The coroner observes to his officer that there has been a mistake in that the inquest has been scheduled on the deceased's birthday. However, his wife had been advised of this and said that she did not want the inquest to be postponed.

There is no announcement of the name of the deceased. The first witness is a police sergeant. It is not clear at this point if any family members are present – there are various people scattered around who may be family or friends, but the coroner makes no acknowledgement of them. The sergeant's evidence comprises a summary of various statements.

The next witness, Adrian Thompson, was driving a car which was overtaken shortly before the accident. He then came upon the accident, caused by the car which had overtaken him. Mr Thompson is defeated by various questions from the coroner about road camber and speed limits. Nonetheless his evidence appears damning of the conduct of the driver involved in the accident. He appears to have been speeding, and Mr Thompson suggests that he went through a red light at a railway crossing just before the barriers descended. Mr Thompson on a number of occasions gives a half laugh and makes odd, inappropriate asides. He is probably nervous.

Next we have Maria Blake, another driver. She came upon the accident just after it had happened. At the end of her evidence, another solicitor (who it turns out is representing Mrs Hughes) asks whether the barriers to the level crossing were down at the point when she witnessed the scene. Apparently they were. Next we have another witness to the accident, Ms Reeves. The coroner's technique is to begin by reading from her statement. When Ms Reeves is asked what speed the car was doing, she replies: "*Too fast basically*". She heard a sickening thud and saw a man tumbling and rolling. The car then stopped. This witness's evidence is most relevant to any criminal charge since she is the only one who actually saw the accident. The solicitor for the driver asks a number of detailed questions about her positioning and what she could see. The burden of his questioning is to try to establish that Ms Reeves could not see the other side of the railway line and therefore could not be confident that at the point the driver of the car drove onto the crossing the lights were in fact red. She acknowledges that she couldn't see the line on the other side of the crossing. Nor could she be certain of the driver's speed.

Next we have the evidence of Mr Clarke, the driver. He is aged about 30. Just as the coroner is to begin questioning him, Mr Clarke's solicitor intervenes to say that he has advised his client not to answer any questions. Mr Clarke confirms this, indicating that on his solicitor's advice he is going to say nothing in response to the coroner's questions. The solicitor says that he would prefer the coroner simply to read from Mr Clarke's statement. In fact the coroner gives up at this point. He doesn't read the statement.

Next we have the evidence of the police constable who interviewed Mr Clarke – one interview lasting ten minutes at the scene, and a further longer interview some time later. He reads from his notes of what Mr Clarke had said to him. The coroner asks the solicitor representing Mrs Hughes whether she wants the whole of the second interview read out. She says that as she hasn't seen it, she doesn't know. In the end the police constable summarises the driver's statement. He also observes that there were no brake marks at the scene. The solicitor asks about stopping distances and the constable imparts a considerable amount of information on this subject. The burden of this is that Mr Clarke could have stopped before striking Mr Hughes had he been travelling at only 30 miles per hour. The constable's manner is confident and assertive. At one point the coroner asks whether .7 of a second (the figure that he has been given) is the average reaction time or whether, on the part of some drivers, it might be a little longer than this. The officer responds: "*It's reasonable to assume that, yes sir*".

There is also a long series of questions from Mr Clarke's solicitor to the police constable. Again it would seem clear that he is preparing the ground for Mr Clarke's trial on the careless driving charge. The point that the solicitor is trying to make is that the damage to the car is on its side and this suggests that Mr Hughes walked into the side of the car (a considerable feat in respect of a vehicle travelling at over 30 mph). The coroner asks why the solicitor is pursuing this line of questioning. He says, rather impatiently, that everyone can see that this is an accident and that the verdict is going to be that Mr Hughes died as a result of a road traffic accident. This, he adds, "*implies no blame against anyone*". The solicitor desists, but observes as he does so that he is sure that the coroner understands the point that he was seeking to establish.

The coroner concludes the inquest. He apologises for the fact that the inquest is held on Mr Hughes's birthday. He stressed that the family wished it to go ahead. Death was the result of a collision with a vehicle, causing multiple injuries. He says he would like to express sympathy to all concerned. (It is difficult to know who in the courtroom is concerned. Two aged gentlemen are seated at the back of the court and leave when this inquest is concluded, so perhaps they were friends of Mr Hughes.)

## Inquest 9
### Paul Scott, Thomas Scott, Katherine Lovell, Simon Morgan
### Court 6, Coroner F

The courtroom, although large, is almost full for this inquest with at least 30 people entering. All are African-Caribbean, very smartly and sombrely dressed, and of assorted ages. The immediate impression is that of a funeral. The inquest is concerned with the deaths of four young people killed in a road traffic accident in Belgium.

We observe the coroner's officer trying to identify various individuals amongst the throng. He talks to two of them. This inquest had been opened four months ago. Two of those who died were brothers, a third was a cousin of theirs, and the fourth was a friend.

The coroner reads from the statement of the mother of the two Scott brothers. Apparently they were born in 1973 and 1974. The Belgian post mortem gave cause of death in each case as a skull fracture. The coroner reads something of the life history of the two boys as reported by their mother. Again, this feels like a mini-funeral oration. One had secured a degree in computers. Both were active members of the Seventh Day Adventist Church. One had been a loving father to his daughter.

Then we have the statement of the father of Katherine Lovell (born 1981). Another funeral oration of sorts. Katherine also suffered a fractured skull and, in addition, a fractured thorax.

Then we have the statement of the mother of Simon Morgan (born 1973). He was a happy lad, etc. Simon had also died of a skull fracture. The coroner looks up and addresses the assembled throng. *"Do I take it that these four young people were all related?"* Somebody answers him: the Scott brothers and Katherine Lovell were cousins; Simon Morgan was a friend of theirs. The atmosphere, just as one might expect, is sombre. Everyone is sitting in complete silence, looking at the coroner.

Then the coroner reads a statement from a witness to the accident – as it happens, an English truck driver. The road was wet. He was overtaken at some speed by a car containing the four deceased. Some 200 yards ahead of him the car skidded and smashed into a bridge. The car was split in two. No other vehicle was involved.

Then the coroner reads from an English translation of the Belgian fatal accident traffic report. The vehicle was a black BMW. They believe (but cannot be sure) that it was being driven by Mark Scott. The four young people were dead at the scene. The road was a motorway with a speed limit of 120 kph. It was night, but the road was lit. The road surface was wet. The vehicle split in two, having collided with a bridge pillar. All four occupants were thrown from the car. No blood samples were taken. No other vehicle was involved. The coroner reads this report at length – perhaps trying to give some value to the extended family massed in front of him. It is said that the two rear tyres of the vehicle were bald.

That, it appears, is the end of the evidence. The coroner sums up: "What should have been a happy holiday turned into a disaster". He says that all four had suffered severe head injuries. Then the coroner fumbles amongst his notes for a moment – there is an embarrassed silence whilst this goes on. Finally he finds what he is looking for and notes that Katherine Lovell had also suffered chest injuries. The coroner says that it is not clear if there was a full post mortem conducted in Belgian, but it is clear what the cause of death was in each case. He expresses his condolences to the family and to all those present. This, the coroner believes and hopes, is the end of the inquest. However, nobody moves. Everyone sits in stunned silence, looking at the coroner. It is evident that they are expecting much more from these proceedings.

It is the coroner's officer who breaks the silence. He goes to speak to the coroner and we hear him say that some family members would like to ask questions. The coroner had not invited questions and he had given no indication that he was expecting any. Then, various members of the family – at first tentatively but then rather more confidently – ask questions of the coroner. They are polite throughout. The mother of Katherine Lovell says she would like to know what happened to her daughter's passport. The coroner says that he doesn't know – perhaps it was destroyed at the scene. Another member of the family – a young man – asks about the truck driver's evidence. He had said that several cars had passed him. Did he say anything about the distance between the vehicles? The coroner checks the statement. It says simply that no other vehicle was involved. The coroner refers at this point to the problems involved in having an inquest in respect of an accident which had occurred abroad. They are fortunate, he says, to have even one English witness.

Then there are questions about the young people's clothing – apparently not returned. The coroner says that he cannot assist in respect of any property. Then there is a question about whether the fractures were incurred before or after the impact with the bridge. At this point the coroner, perhaps concluding that this questioning is likely to continue for some time, says to the assembled throng that he has finished taking evidence now and the inquest is concluded. In any event, as he puts it, "*I can't give evidence to my own court*". Nevertheless he then elaborates somewhat on the accident itself, observing that tremendous forces must have been applied when the vehicle overturned and hit the bridge in order for it to have split in two. It is impossible to say at what point the injuries were sustained.

The questions persist. The mother of the two Scott brothers asks why they kept the bodies in hospital for several days, and then why, having kept the bodies, they did not after all conduct a post mortem. She says, plaintively, "*Then we heard that nothing was done ... By that time it was too late for us to view our children ... It was too late for us to hold them.*"

The coroner apparently decides that he cannot go on trying to respond to questions of this kind (to which he doesn't know the answer) whilst facing this multitude of grieving faces. He decides to move to the round table in the well of the courtroom. It seats about six. He asks whether representatives of each branch of the family might like to join him at this table to continue the discussion. This is indeed what happens. Rather tentatively, various members of the family are singled out, or single themselves out, and descend to the table in the well of the court where the coroner has now placed himself. Chairs are moved to accommodate about six people round the table.

At first the focus is on what happened to the young people's bodies when they arrived at the UK airport. It is difficult to hear this conversation very well because all those not present around the table are seated some distance away. It is a bit of theatre, but none of the actors is taking the trouble to project their voice.

Mrs Lovell asks a question about the identification of her daughter. She suspects that some of the facial injuries her daughter sustained were incurred after the accident, after she had been identified. Unfortunately there are no medical witnesses, so it is not possible for the coroner to respond effectively to the concern which she has expressed. The coroner does his best: he says he doesn't believe that the bodies would have been tampered with – after all, the investigators had established a clear cause of death.

At this point another member of the family is invited down to the table at which this discussion is taking place. He had tried to intervene and so the coroner invites him to join them. This gentleman explains that it was he who organised the repatriation of the bodies. The coroner observes at one point that there was no need for a further post mortem. If that had been required the bodies would have gone to the local hospital – but in fact they were never sent there. Why, he was asked, were the bodies not released at that point? The coroner replies that he did not at that stage have confirmation of identities and an established cause of death. Once he had those he was able to open the inquest and allow the funerals to go ahead. He says to all and sundry: "*We never say that people cannot see bodies; but we sometimes advise that it may not be advisable*". The coroner hypothesises that the injuries which Katherine Lovell and the others had suffered may have progressed beyond the point when they were first witnessed by another family member as a result of the delay in embalming. There is then a protracted discussion of how this kind of deterioration can occur, and also an discussion of the reasons why there was this delay in embalming.

Whilst all this is going on, everyone else sits around patiently. It is an extraordinary atmosphere, extremely sombre. What is also evident, however, is that there is a huge appetite for information which has not yet been satisfied. This is perhaps because the deaths in this case were so tragic – four young people, in the prime of life. The stunned reaction seems in keeping with that.

Someone raises the question of the allegedly bald tyres. Apparently they had sought information about this, but it had been denied them by the Belgian authorities. There is a query as to whether bald really means bald, as against close to the limit. Somebody asks whether sketches of the accident can be made available to them. The coroner replies: "*You are entitled to a copy of absolutely everything*". It is suggested that in fact the tyres weren't bald – the accident report said that they had a depth of three millimetres, whereas an MOT test demands only two millimetres. The coroner says that it would be necessary to consult the Belgian police directly on this point: "*These things are never satisfactory. We can't wait three years to hold an inquest – we've got this thing (he is referring to the translation of the Belgian police report) which gives a basic impression.*" One family member asks whether they couldn't have had the person responsible for the accident report present at the inquest. There, perhaps, is the nub. The families would have liked to have present whoever it was who conducted the police and the medical examinations in Belgium. As it is these key figures are not present and we have to rely on whatever the coroner and the coroner's officer have gleaned.

The coroner sees the point, and has the courage to address it. He says that he could have asked the accident investigator to be present, but he couldn't compel him to attend without going through a complex legal procedure. He explains that he felt there was nothing that he could do, specifically in relation to possible recommendations. Anyway, we are dealing with Belgian traffic regulations and (he implies) there's not much point in an English coroner commenting on Belgian speed limits. Anyway, for these reasons the coroner says that he decided that it was not appropriate for him to seek the attendance of the Belgian traffic investigator.

By now this post-inquest question and answer session has lasted for some 45 minutes. No one has moved. There are signs that the coroner is reaching the end of his tether. He has been as receptive as he can, but clearly he doesn't want this to go on much longer. He tries to bring everyone back to the verdict – which, he explains, is not in doubt; also … "as I can't influence anything further in Belgium", back to the limitations of the inquest process.

After about 50 minutes of this (strictly speaking, post-inquest) question and answer session, we appear to be running out of steam. Then the questions suddenly pick up again. Some family members are concerned about the timing of the issuing of the death certificate. It is clear that they are still trying to make sense of the whole thing. They want to use the deaths of their children, as one of them says, "to stop various things". Reference is made to the fact that the road on which the accident occurred is (they believe) a notorious accident black-spot. So they are trying to make a difference – to get something positive out of the deaths of their children.

As for the 25 or so family members who are not privy to this discussion around the table in the well of the court, they show amazing patience. It must be rather frustrating, only being able to catch the odd word or two. We [researchers] are closer to the action than most, and even we are finding it difficult to follow what is going on.

The discussion concludes with the family asking if they can have copies of all the materials, all the accident reports, all the statements. The coroner says that they can have a photocopy of everything. And so we end, and the family troop out, still with a palpable air of sadness.

Some time afterwards we talk to one of those present – Mr Reynolds, an uncle of the two Scott brothers who died. He recognised that the coroner had made an effort in, effectively, stepping out of role and engaging in the long discussion with family representatives. He said that the family had wanted an explanation of what had happened leading up to the accident – exactly how and why their children had died. The inquest did not provide them with anything like the level of explanation that they were seeking. They had been looking to the inquest to answer all their questions. They thought that the lorry driver should have been present. He was a key witness and he was, after all, English. Also, the copy of the accident report which they had received was untranslated. They were still themselves waiting for a translated copy – something which they had arranged at their own initiative. The accident investigator should have been another key witness. But neither he nor the lorry driver was present (although Mr Reynolds acknowledged that it may have been difficult for the coroner to require the attendance of Belgian investigators).

The family had been totally devastated by their loss. The parents had visited the site of the accident in Belgium, and they had also gone to the garage where the wreck of the car was housed. It was very distressing for them that the children's personal effects were just gathered together and left in a bag in a warehouse. Their children's blood was still clearly visible on their effects.

Mr Reynolds also commented that there had been inadequate liaison with the coroner prior to the inquest. The family had not been asked who they thought should give evidence at the inquest. Nor had they been asked who they themselves would like to put forward to give evidence. As Mr Reynolds put it, the feeling that they'd had was that the coroner was in charge, and that's it. There had also been a good deal of confusing and conflicting information regarding what had happened to the young people's bodies. First they'd been told by the coroner's officer that they could not see the bodies because they were being held by the coroner who would require there to be a post mortem. In fact no post mortem was conducted in this country, but by the time the parents were allowed to see their children, eight to ten days had passed and their bodies had deteriorated. In particular, their faces were distorted. This was a cause of further distress. All this had happened before the inquest and so they had been looking to the inquest to provide not only an explanation not only of the accident, but also of the chain of events which followed.

The family had also wanted to get to the bottom of exactly who was involved in the accident. This opportunity was denied them. For example, they believed that there were video cameras on the motorway – had these been studied? Was anyone else involved? On that point they certainly would have liked to have heard from the lorry driver. Why did the car lose control? As Mr Reynolds put it: "We wanted to know the full story – the real story of exactly how they died". As it was, they did not believe that much effort was expended on the case by the Belgian traffic investigators and then, within the inquest process, they did not believe that much effort was expended by the coroner or his staff. It was important for the family to understand everything about what had happened. For example, the question of who was driving was all part of the story of the accident. As it was, they still didn't know. The family also wanted to know the accident record on this stretch of motorway. Were accidents there a regular occurrence? As Mr Reynolds said again, this was all part of the story.

He did give the coroner credit for the empathy which he had shown in being willing to continue to talk to the family. That was appreciated. But the investigation as a whole was inadequate. It had the effect of making the parents and the other family members feel as if the children's lives had been cheapened.

The family was also concerned about the issue of race. Here we had three young black males and a young black female travelling in a country – Belgium – which was not known for its sympathetic approach to black people. The family had the feeling that the cursory treatment of the deaths may in part have been because the young people were black. They were not, as he put it, four white medical students from Oxford University. They were four black kids with music playing … driving a fast car … in other words, not the kind of people and the kind of circumstances which would necessarily galvanise investigators. Nor the kind of people who would necessarily galvanise a coroner.

The family was still struggling to come to terms with what had happened. They had looked to the inquest to provide an end to their uncertainty. As it was, there was a huge gap between the family's expectations of the inquest and what had actually been provided. This was despite the coroner's best efforts on the day. They had emerged from the inquest with a massive sense of disappointment.


## Inquest 10
**James Fraser**
**Court 2, Coroner B**

This is the third inquest of a morning session that is running slightly late. The main area of seating for the public is on the right hand side of the courtroom and Mr Carter, rider of the motorcycle that killed James, is sitting on the left of this area, accompanied by a female friend and a man who takes notes throughout the proceedings. Mr Fraser, James's father, is sitting on the far right. Before the inquest starts a coroner's officer orders Mr Carter and Mr Fraser to swap seats. On the left-hand side of the courtroom sit two police officers and Mr Wilson, a coach driver and witness to this sudden death. At the front of the court beneath the coroner's podium are two solicitors. One is representing Mr Carter, the other is representing Mrs Cope, James's mother. Also present are several members of the press.

The coroner enters and starts the inquest. The acoustics are very poor, so it is not possible to hear everything that he is saying. He also speaks softly. He gives the date when the inquest was first opened (six months previously) and runs through the list of intended witnesses, observing: "*I will have Mr Fraser's statement read rather than have him give evidence*".

The coroner summarises the evidence of the neural pathologist who undertook James's post mortem. James had multiple injuries, including injuries to his leg and spine. The cause of death was traumatic brain damage. Death would have occurred soon after the injuries were inflicted.

The coroner then calls the first witness, Mr Wilson, the coach driver. Mr Wilson describes driving his coach along a main road in the early evening. He noticed an adult and some children on bicycles attempting to cross the road. A motorcyclist, going in the opposite direction, passed the coach. Mr Wilson looked in his mirror, concerned as to whether the motorcyclist would see the party crossing the road as there was a high hedgerow that created a blind spot in the road. As he looked in his mirror he saw that there was a cyclist in the road. The motorcyclist crashed into the cyclist. The cyclist was thrown into the air and the motorbike skidded along the road on its side. The coroner and Mr Wilson have in front of them photographs which show the road layout and which aid Mr Wilson's description of events.

The coroner asks the solicitors whether they have any questions. Both of them do. The solicitor representing Mr Carter asks Mr Wilson about his view of the road, his distance from the accident, Mr Carter's likely view of the road, the height of the hedgerow, the position of the sun, and the curvature of the road. The solicitor representing Mrs Cope also questions Mr Wilson on distance, and his view of the road. He also asks whether Mr Carter's headlamp was on, and about the speed he was travelling. The two solicitors have several 'goes' at questioning Mr Wilson. At first Mr Wilson answers these questions in a co-operative manner. However, as the questioning continues his manner gradually changes and he appears increasingly defensive. By the time the two solicitors have finished with their questions he seems tired and rather angry.

The coroner then asks his officer to read Mr Fraser's statement. Mr Fraser and his three sons had cycled to their aunt's house. They were on their way back, cycling along country roads. They arrived at a junction, where they prepared to cross a busy main road. They were used to doing this in stages, with Mr Fraser telling the children when they should cross. Usually the two eldest children went first. Then Mr Fraser would cross with his youngest child. He signalled that it was safe to cross. His eldest son crossed the road safely, and waited at the other side. Mr Fraser then heard a buzzing noise, then saw a motorcycle coming towards them. He turned to look at his two other sons and realised that James had started to cross the road. He shouted, "*Stop!*" James had reached the middle of the road by this point and stopped, straddling the white lines in the middle of the road with his bike. The motorbike then hit him. He was thrown into the air and landed on the other side of the road.

The coroner then asks the officer to read the statements of James's two brothers. Their accounts are very similar to that of Mr Fraser except there is some additional dialogue. Someone, they were not sure who, said, "*Okay, it is clear*" before the eldest son crossed the road. Just before the motorbike hit James, James shouted "*Daddy!*".

The next witness to be called is the police constable who attended the scene of James's death. He describes the positions of the motorbike, the bicycle and James.

A police accident investigator then gives evidence. He describes the layout of the road and the condition of the motorcycle, which was in good working order. He calculates the speed at which James would have walked his bike across the road. He also calculates the speed of the motorcyclist as being 74 mph. The speed limit on this road is 60 mph. The motorcyclist's light was probably not switched on. Whilst the accident investigator gives this evidence Mr Carter becomes rather agitated. His girlfriend comforts him. Each solicitor questions the accident investigator on how he arrived at his conclusions. The solicitor for Mr Carter asks the most questions. How has he come to the conclusion that the lamp was not switched on? What was the state of the road, the position of the sun, the height of the obscuring hedgerow (which it transpires was cut down very soon after the accident)? The solicitor for Mrs Cope asks how he calculated the speed of a child crossing a road, and how he arrived at a figure of 74 mph for the speed of the motorbike. The questioning is quite protracted.

The accident investigator then gives evidence concerning an interview he conducted with Mr Carter, at his solicitor's office. Here Mr Carter claimed that his bike headlamp was switched on. He also denied that he was speeding. His son was riding pillion, and he was concerned for his safety. The statement described how he came round a bend and saw James too late to be able to avoid him. Mr Carter had lost consciousness briefly and he and his son were slightly injured.

Mr Carter then gives evidence. The coroner is reassuring: "*You are not on trial. That is not the object of the inquiry.*" The coroner adds that he does not want to prejudice proceedings taking place elsewhere. His questioning is perfunctory – confirming identity and verifying the statement given to the police officer. Mr Carter divulges little about his experience of the crash.

The coroner then briefly sums up. He says this was "*an accidental death following a road traffic accident*". He further observes that "*this case is tragic for all involved*". He leaves the courtroom.

Mr Fraser was interviewed some five months later. He is divorced from Mrs Cope, James's mother. His perception was that the investigating officer had treated Mrs Cope as James's next-of-kin. He suspected that this was linked to her employment (she is a solicitor). This irked him: "*The children were in my care at the time and I would have thought I was a responsible adult there. So I should really be the point of reference for what was going on ... rather than 'Oh, we've told your wife about this and now we're letting you know'.*"

He felt that there had been a long gap between James's death and the inquest. The waiting was not helped by the knowledge that there was also to be a criminal prosecution of the driver.

Before the inquest the police investigator had been to visit Mr Fraser. Mr Fraser commented that "*the policeman was at pains to stress that the inquest was to find out the cause of death and nothing else, not to assign blame. Tricky one that.*" The police officer went through the evidence with him.

As well as the pending criminal prosecution of the motorcyclist, Mrs Cope was contemplating a civil action. Mr Fraser observed: "*I think obviously part of, half of, the difficulty with her situation is that she apportioned blame towards me as well. Because I was in charge of the children. And, well, an accident like that shouldn't have happened. She obviously blames me. She blames the motorcyclist as well, but she blames me.*" Mr Fraser also blamed himself.

Mr Fraser said that his ex-wife "*wants the children to appear in court, or is willing for them to appear in court, to give evidence. Whereas I would prefer them not to. Because it is traumatic enough for them to see the whole thing, let alone to have to relive it. ... The only difference it is going to make to anyone is financial. So I have been out on a limb on that.*" He also referred to the impending prosecution of Mr Carter as something that was hanging over him, an event he was not looking forward to. This trial had itself been subject to various delays.

James's mother did not attend the inquest. Mr Fraser said: "*She knew what to expect and she felt she couldn't cope with it, so she didn't go, didn't want to know about it.*" Instead, she had focused her attention on the criminal prosecution of the driver, and her possible civil action against him. Mr Fraser described his ex-wife as a litigation lawyer who specialised in personal injury claims. He felt that her professional status gave her more power in this situation. With respect to the inquest, Mr Fraser thought the coroner had been "*at pains not to worry the motorcyclist more than anything else*". He thought that "*it was a trifle strange that the chap who was facing charges was two yards to my right*".

Mr Fraser was concerned about the evidence of Mr Wilson, the coach driver: "*There were a number of inaccuracies in what was said that weren't dealt with. Now I know it wasn't trying to apportion blame in any way, but I was surprised that they weren't picked up. I mean they are of no consequence to me, it doesn't make any difference. But I just felt that if they were going to the trouble of bringing all these people here, at least they could get the correct facts... The coroner seemed quite prepared to accept a, I'd say, fairly wishy-washy picture of the road, of what the road looked like, and its state... He seemed quite willing to accept a fairly 'that's about right' sort of aspect.*" Accordingly he felt that the court had not dealt with facts, but rather opinion. He added: "*I didn't feel it necessary to intervene because it was only an inquest after all*". He linked these inaccuracies to the presence of solicitors. "*The point was, one of them felt that the blame was going in an area that it shouldn't be going. So out came the photographs...*" Inaccuracy had arisen because the proceedings became adversarial.

Mr Fraser had found the inquest useful in that "*it probably gave me an insight into the way the court case was going to go*". It also had a cathartic effect: "*I suppose the only reason I went there was that I knew I was responsible. So I had to go through that process … It was useful to me. I mean, if it had involved seven days, I'd have been there. I'd have sat through it, whatever, because I felt it was necessary for me to do it.*"

But, in terms of the content of the inquest, he was critical. He could not see the point of all the detail. "*Either he was killed by a motorcycle in an accident, or he wasn't. The cause of death was the fact that he got hit by a motorcycle, going too fast. We all knew that. So why go into the rest of the palaver?*" He realised that the inquest was necessary for the public record, but he wondered: "*Can you have degrees of inquest? Can you have an inquest of an elderly person who dies in their sleep in their bed? And, of course you have no interest in that, but presumably you have to go through the same performance.*" He would have liked to have seen less detail, including less about the post mortem. "*The inquest is simply to establish the cause of death. It could have been done a week later, or two weeks later, I don't know. …But if it is just to find the cause of death, all they needed was photographs, bits and pieces on the situation of the road, and a few basic details. Obviously they want the post-mortem result as well. And that's it. What else do they need if that is all an inquest is for? But maybe that's not all it is for.*"

## Inquest 11
### Lee Sharpe
### Court 8, Coroner G

This is the third inquest of the morning. A number of trainee police officers have been sitting in the courtroom throughout. They are observing inquests as a part of their training. Two police officers involved in this case sit at the side of the room. A reporter sits at the front of the court beneath the coroner's podium.

The coroner's officer brings in the family members. They are a large crowd, probably about 20 in number. The coroner's officer announces that this is the inquest for Lee Sharpe. The coroner explains to the family that there is a missing witness, a Mr Bourke. He says: "*I am in the family's hands ... If the family want, we can stop and try and get him here – not today though. Or we can see how we go. His evidence isn't central.*" Some family members nod and murmur apparent agreement. The coroner decides to carry on.

The first witness is Debbie Miller. The coroner asks: "*You were Lee's partner, but you split up with him four weeks before he died?*" Debbie agrees. The coroner asks leading questions based on Debbie's statement. "*You were with Lee for 22 years. You had two children. The relationship was quite volatile*". Debbie agrees with all this. Lee had been dependent on heroin in the past, but he was not using heroin at the time of his death. Debbie says that Lee had not taken heroin for three years. The coroner asks if alcohol was a problem. Debbie affirms that it was. The coroner says that sometimes alcohol problems develop after people give up heroin. "*Was that the case with him?*" "*Yes.*"

"*Did he ever speak about taking his life?*" Debbie answers: "*Yes, frequently over the last four months or so*". The coroner asks: "*Did you take it seriously?*" Debbie replies: "*Not until when he said how he would do it*".

The coroner then asks Debbie to tell the court when she last saw Lee. Debbie launches into a narrative. She saw Lee the Saturday before he died. (He was certified dead on the Sunday.) "*He came round at 4.00 p.m. to collect some ice. He was going to his cousin's house. He asked me if he could have a shower. My daughter, who is 14, had gone out with a friend. I loved him to pieces but I couldn't live with him.*" Debbie tends to offer some factual information but then inserts a commentary on her feelings for Lee. She is trying to explain to the court aspects of their relationship. The coroner interrupts her when this happens.

Lee returned to the house again. He was in a distressed state and demanded money and jewellery. He went upstairs. He had razorblades on him, which he used to slash Debbie's clothes. Debbie then tells the court that Lee wanted to have sex with her that night. The coroner says: "*Really, you don't have to tell us this!*" The police were called and managed to defuse the situation.

The next day Debbie's daughter was worried about her father. Debbie drove round with her to the house where Lee was staying. Lee didn't answer the door. Then Debbie saw Lee's silhouette in the front downstairs bedroom, and saw that he had hanged himself. The coroner asks: "*Was he dead?*" "Yes." The coroner asks if there was a suicide note. "*No.*" The coroner then invites questions from the family. There aren't any.

The coroner then reads a report from Lee's GP. There was no sign of psychiatric problems. Lee had used heroin up to 1995, then methadone. The GP had not seen Lee since 1996.

Next to give evidence is Debbie's boyfriend, Mark. He seems very ill at ease and mumbles. He tells the court that he had known Lee for about four years. Lee was extremely distressed. The coroner asks whether Mark had seen Lee with a knife. "*Yes.*" "*Did he say what he would do with it?*" "*No.*" The coroner then asks: "*Did you think he was at risk?*" Mark replies: "*No, not at the time. But now I think about it…*"

Mark says that Lee had told him the night before he died: "*I'm not going to kill myself over you*". When Mark says this, there is a sound from the middle rows, where Lee's family is seated. An older woman, who may be Lee's mother, starts to cry.

The police constable, who arrived at the scene of the incident at Debbie's house, gives his evidence. He states that this was a potential siege situation.

The coroner then reads the statement of the missing witness, Ronald Bourke. Mr Bourke's statement is quite brief. He had known Lee since they were children and they were good friends. Lee was staying at his flat, sleeping on the sofa in the front room because he was having matrimonial problems.

There are two further witnesses – Debbie's brother-in-law and the police constable who attended the scene of the death. Once the police constable has given his evidence the coroner turns to the post mortem and toxicology report. The toxicology report shows that Lee had over twice the permitted alcohol level for driving in his blood. This, the coroner says, gives some idea of his intoxication levels. The medical cause of death was 'suspension'.

The coroner then asks the family if they want to go ahead with the conclusion of the inquest. They say they do. The coroner says that this event has soured what had been a largely happy life. He hopes that once the inquest is concluded the family will be able to grieve and these events will fade. He says: "*Death was due to suspension. Lee killed himself whilst the balance of his mind was disturbed. I think he was very distressed at the time. It would not have been a painful death at all, but that isn't something we advertise.*" Several of Lee's family members are tearful as they leave the court.

Debbie Miller was interviewed by telephone some three months later. The inquest had been a great ordeal for her. A female coroner's officer showed her round the courtroom and explained things … "*but my legs turned to jelly*". However, the coroner's officer was a very caring woman and made her feel calmer. Nonetheless "*having to go through it all again*" was very difficult … "*All those emotions. I was frightened I would start crying. If I started I wouldn't stop.*" She also found it difficult to sit through the evidence given by her brother-in-law and her boyfriend, where they described how they had forced an entry and cut Lee's body down from where it was hanging.

Debbie thought that the inquest "*had to be done, to determine what and why*". She had agreed with the coroner's conclusion that Lee was unbalanced. "*The night before he died he cut my telephone wires with a razor-blade.*" He had also told her, some weeks before, that he wanted to end his life.

Debbie was left with one concern. Lee smoked cannabis. The post mortem report stated that there was only a minor quantity of cocaine in Lee's system. Debbie said: "*I couldn't understand how it never showed up. I was going to ask, and kept thinking, should I, shouldn't I?*" She believed that Lee may also have started using heroin again.

Debbie had felt intimidated by Lee's family at the inquest and this was one reason she didn't mention the drugs, or ask drug-related questions. The whole inquest was very nerve-racking for her because Lee's family had turned against her after his death. They blamed her. She had split up with Lee four weeks prior to his death, and started going out with his friend, Mark. The experience of attending the inquest with Lee's family as a hostile audience was very difficult for her.

Her poor relationship with Lee's family was exacerbated by the fact that she and Lee had never married. She had no right to arrange Lee's funeral, and the family had excluded her from a number of mourning events. "*Everything I did, they went over me.*" However, at the inquest she enjoyed the support of her side of the family. When the coroner asked if anyone had any questions, it was Debbie's family who had answered "no". Whilst she had welcomed this acknowledgement, she was still dissatisfied by the outcome of the inquest. "*I wanted them to say whether he had taken heroin.*" Because of her unanswered questions Debbie said she found it difficult to move forward. She regretted her lack of preparation for the inquest: "*On the day I wasn't too clever about it. I should have taken some notes on a piece of paper.*" If the coroner had produced a written report of the inquest and given it to her, this would have helped. She would also have liked to have read some of the statements beforehand, to prepare her for what she was going to hear.

## Inquest 12
### Edith Spencer
### Court 7, Coroner C

This is a specially designed coroner's court. It is small and relatively informal, although rather cramped. The area in which the coroner sits is not raised, and thus the coroner appears more accessible than in some of the larger courtrooms. The coroner's officer announces to all and sundry: "*We are very informal here ... not like the magistrates' court, more like a family*".

Edith Spencer died nine months ago. The coroner summarises the evidence. Edith was found dead at 7 a.m. by a nursing auxiliary at the nursing home where she was a resident. She was found sitting on a toilet with a plastic bag over her head. The pathologist concludes that death was the result of suffocation by the plastic bag. A note was found in Edith's handwriting. The coroner refers to the pathologist's report. He says: "*I don't read all of this out, for obvious reasons*".

The first witness is a nursing auxiliary. Through leading questions the coroner establishes that her job was to wake the residents in the nursing home. Edith had been resident for about a month. When the nurse went to wake her that morning she saw that she was not in her bed. She went to the en suite bathroom and saw Edith sitting bent over with a plastic bag on her head, the bag being secured with a dressing gown belt. The coroner offers the family an opportunity to ask questions, which they decline.

The coroner then calls the deputy matron to the witness stand. She explains that Edith had suffered a fall, following which she had returned to her flat for one night, but was unable to cope and so had returned to the main house. She says that Edith had seemed more cheerful than over the previous three or four days. She had no knowledge that she was planning to take her own life. Again the family are asked if they have any questions, and again they decline this offer. Rose Spencer, Edith's niece, then takes the stand. She tells the coroner quite firmly: "*I am the next-of-kin*". The coroner asks whether Edith had been in low spirits. Rose replies: "*She was more than in low spirits, she was depressed*". Rose says that there were "*multiple reasons*" for this. The coroner offers Rose an opportunity to read the note which was left by Edith. Rose takes the note and reads it to herself.

The coroner then asks: "*When you last saw your aunt, was she anxious to get back to her flat?*" Rose does not reply to this question. Instead she says: "*You asked about her depression. She was in severe pain after a fall. The x-ray showed a fractured pelvis. I'd like to know what the x-ray report said, and the date the x-ray was taken.*" The coroner seems taken aback: "*I am not sure I can answer that*". Rose responds: "*It's a crucial question*". The coroner turns to the deputy matron for help: "*Do you know about the fracture?*" The deputy matron replies firmly that there were no fractures visible on the x-ray. There then follows an exchange between Rose and the deputy matron. Eventually Brian Spencer, Edith's brother, intervenes from the well of the court: "*Rose, my sister said she had a cracked pelvis as a result of the fall. She said that she'd been told that there was no cure, that she just had to wait.*" Rose responds to the effect that an x-ray had indeed been taken and that her aunt was "*in pain ... acute pain*".

The coroner's patience is evidently being tried by these exchanges. At one point he says: "*It would have been helpful if these questions had been articulated before, rather than now, so I could address them. This is not really a matter for an inquest.*" There follow further exchanges between Rose Spencer and the deputy matron, with the coroner acting as referee. Eventually he intervenes again: "*I am going to adjourn for a few minutes and talk to my officer*".

After the coroner has left the court Rose returns to her seat and talks to the deputy matron. There is a good deal of whispering and at one point Rose proclaims loudly: "*There should be a doctor here with the results of the x-ray*".

The coroner returns and asks the family generally: "*Did any of you have concerns about the treatment by the doctor or the home?*" Brian Spencer responds, referring to his sister's drugs régime and to her depression. The coroner has heard enough. He says that he proposes to adjourn and call for a medical report on Edith's fracture and on her depression. Brian Spencer counters: "*But she was prescribed pills for depression. She wouldn't take them. She said, 'I know what's depressing me, so I don't need them'.*" The coroner says to his officer: "*We need to take a statement from Mr Spencer*". He seems exasperated: "*I think we should deal with the post mortem and then adjourn. This means weeks of delay.*".

The coroner summarises the post mortem evidence, with its conclusion that death was the result of plastic bag suffocation. He sums up: "*In reality, I have heard enough evidence to allow me to conclude, but due to the concerns raised I will get reports on the medical x-ray, the depression, the home's nursing records, plus a statement from Mr Spencer*". He turns to Rose Spencer and says sympathetically: "*I hope this will answer your concerns*".

After the coroner and the relatives have departed, the deputy matron is tearful. The police officer comforts her.

Later the coroner tells us that he is frustrated that Rose Spencer did not raise her concerns earlier. He felt he should adjourn because these were such fundamental issues. The purpose of the inquest is in part to make the family feel better and to answer their questions. He feels that the adjournment will help Rose. He says that her questions are not strictly within the jurisdiction of the court and she shouldn't use the forum of the inquest to raise them. Nonetheless in the long run it will be easier to adjourn, get all the evidence in, and finish off the inquest in a few weeks' time.

The inquest is resumed three weeks later. This time there seems to be considerable tension within the Spencer family. Edith's brother and sister-in-law sit with their niece, whilst Rose Spencer is seated in another part of the courtroom.

Opening the resumed inquest the coroner firmly sets out the purposes of the inquest. This hearing is more coherent and goes into much greater detail. A considerable body of evidence has been collected concerning Edith's medical history. As the coroner takes the witnesses through their evidence he constructs a narrative of the few weeks immediately preceding Edith's death. She was a strong-willed lady, determined and sometimes difficult, who was depressed by her immobility and lack of independence following a fall which resulted in a fractured pelvis. She was depressed at having to live in an institution.

The coroner refers to the case of *Jamieson* in considering the issue of possible institutional neglect. He says that he is satisfied that there is no evidence of neglect having contributed to Edith Spencer's death. He concludes that she took her own life. He says: "*I am grateful to all the witnesses for assisting me in their various ways. I am impressed by the independence of Edith Spencer and extend sympathy to all the family.*"

Edith's brother, Brian Spencer, was interviewed with his wife some eight months after the inquest was concluded. Brian's main point was that he had been very unhappy at the delay of nine months between Edith's death and the holding of the inquest. He observed: "*Evidence goes stale ... you forget. I was lucky that I made notes at the time.*"

Having said that, he agreed with the coroner's decision to adjourn: "*We all groaned, but there were questions unanswered so I am sure it was right to adjourn*". He said that had the coroner decided not to adjourn that would have been acceptable to him, but that Rose would have felt that she had not had a fair hearing. "*There would not have been facts brought out that should have been brought out. That is the coroner's job. You can't get this anywhere else. The home was under suspicion.*"

Brian thought that Rose had been placed in a very difficult position. She was concerned that there had been negligence on the part of the nursing home: "*Rose is a nurse, and I think she felt that it was up to her, that she had an obligation to raise her concerns*". Brian for his part felt that there were some things that could have led one to criticise the home, "*but nothing to go to town on*". Brian's view was that Edith was often critical and tended only to see her own point of view. She was used to being in charge, having been a manager in her professional life. However, the family believed that there were times when Edith did have good cause to complain. He for his part did not always agree with Rose's reading of events, particularly with her criticism of the home, but he supported the use of the legal system to discover why it was that his sister had come to take her own life. He had read in a leaflet he had picked up at court that the inquest was not designed to apportion blame. He thought that there was a contradiction in this because if there were some blame involved, for example neglect, the inquest would have to identify this.

Brian concluded: "*When we resumed the inquest I thought the home came out of it quite well. There was a log of what Edith was like, the drugs given and when. The evidence was quite good.*" Both Brian and his wife felt that the second inquest was "*very well done*". Brian had no criticisms of the coroner: "*It was done sensitively, yet it was businesslike. The coroner's officer was also excellent. He was an old-fashioned chap. I imagine he is a retired policeman. I remember him saying: 'Our aim is to achieve friendly formality.' He was kindly but authoritative, a no-nonsense approach but very feeling and understanding.*" Of the coroner, he said: "*He did it very well. He plodded through it. He was a bit ponderous, but he had to go through it all. He was polite. A nice chap. He achieved his friendly formality. He mildly ticked off Rose, but he was very kind.*" His wife added: "*Rose could have gone on for ever, but he gave her enough time*".

Brian and his wife felt that the family had benefited from the inquest into Edith's death. They felt that it drew a line and enabled them to move forward. Even Rose had moved forward. They stressed that there was no bad feeling within the family over the inquest.

## Inquest 13
**Daniel Evans**
**Court 5, Coroner E**

This is a jury inquest. The sole next-of-kin is Daniel's mother, who is elderly and too frail to attend. Accordingly, there is no family representation.

Daniel died some five months ago. He was serving a life sentence. The coroner addresses the jury: "You may wonder why you are here. Under the Coroners Act, if I have cause to suspect someone has died a violent or sudden or unnatural death in prison, then I must summon a jury."

The coroner goes on to explain the purposes of the inquest: "It is to investigate in public things that should be investigated in public. Even if someone dies a natural death in prison, the coroner must investigate. There is good reason for this. Those in prison are dependent on others for their welfare. The inquest is there to remove suspicion, to get to the facts and avoid rumour from ignorance of facts. It is there to give consolation to families."

Some members of the jury appear to be listening attentively. Others look vaguely bewildered. Several have already switched off. The coroner lists the evidence that will be presented: the background to the case will be given by a coroner's officer. There will be a statement from a fellow prisoner; the result of the post mortem; and the statement of the prison officer who discovered Daniel in his cell.

A coroner's officer takes the stand. Daniel's death was reported to the local police station on the day he died. He was a 41 year old single man. The coroner's officer then reads the statement of Mr Robbins, who was a friend of Daniel and a fellow inmate. Daniel was known as Dan, but he was often referred to as 'Deaf Dan' because he was deaf. On the day that Daniel died Mr Robbins had seen him leaning over the top wing landing. He had asked him in sign language if he was OK. Dan signed that he was OK – a thumbs up – but he also signed that he was ill. It was too far away to read his lips, but he seemed to be signing that he was tired, or had a headache – Mr Robbins wasn't sure which. Perhaps it was both.

The coroner then calls Dr Ahmed, the prison doctor. He reads from the report he compiled some ten days after Daniel's death. This was a death in custody of a 41 year old male who was HIV positive. He had been receiving anti-viral medication. Nine months before his death he had experienced palpitations. He attended a local hospital as an outpatient and was examined by a cardiologist. The cardiologist could find no evidence of heart disease. Two months before he died, Daniel had been diagnosed with oral thrush. Also, he had been examined by a psychiatrist, on secondment to the prison. The psychiatrist had diagnosed depression. He had advised an increase in the anti-depressant medication which Daniel was already taking.

Dr Ahmed had been working in another prison when he was summoned to attend to Daniel. When he arrived he found Daniel face down, facing the door, head by the window. There was a pool of blood, and Daniel was already cold, with rigor mortis setting in. Dr Ahmed pronounced him dead. At this point the coroner asks about the anti-viral medication. Dr Ahmed explains that Daniel was taking this medicine because he was immune-compromised.

Next we have the evidence of the pathologist. He had performed a post mortem on Daniel. Daniel had been suffering from chronic heart disease, with 80 per cent narrowing of the arteries. This could happen naturally. He had died of acute heart failure and coronary artery thrombosis. He was also HIV positive. The pathologist explains that the anti-viral therapy that Daniel was receiving could be linked with coronary sclerosis and thus may have contributed to his death. The coroner observes that Daniel died from 'natural causes'.

Then we have the evidence of the prison officer who had discovered Daniel. He and two other officers were responsible for 64 inmates. At 1400 hours he was on exercise duty. Then he was asked to go to Daniel's cell by a civilian workman. The workman needed access to the cell, had knocked on the cell door, but could get no answer. Because he was deaf, Daniel was in the habit of closing his cell door and putting his bed across the doorway. This meant that he would be woken up by anyone entering the cell. The prison officer tried to gain entry and eventually forced the door. Daniel's head was hanging down over the bed and he was cold and stiff. The coroner asks: "Had he made any report that he was unwell to the authorities?" The officer replies: "Not to my knowledge". At the conclusion of this evidence the coroner asks the members of the jury if they have any questions. They do not. The prison officer steps down.

The coroner begins his summing up: "This was a 41 year old man, who was deaf, had HIV, and was on anti-viral medication. He was seen by a consultant cardiologist and nothing sinister was found. On the day he died a fellow prisoner used sign language to ask him how he was. He gave a thumbs up sign, but indicated that he was feeling unwell and tired. He didn't seem to be in any distress or pain. He was discovered in his cell, lying on his bed. I think you'll agree – it is for you to decide of course – that the evidence we have heard suggests he died of natural causes. You need to look at the balance of evidence and if there *is not sufficient evidence for a verdict of natural causes then you are free to bring in an open verdict. I think on this evidence this will be your conclusion – although it is up to you. It is possible that you may not need to go out to discuss this?"* He looks at the jury for some indication and then says to them: *"I'll ask the foreman to quietly consult … if there are any questions, please ask".*

The members of the jury turn to each other and by various nods and whispers indicate that there is no need for them to retire. They then whisper again to each other, presumably exchanging verdicts. The coroner asks the foreman: *"Has the jury reached a verdict?"* The foreman replies: *"Yes. He died of natural causes."* The coroner asks: *"Is this the verdict of you all?"* The foreman answers: *"Yes".*

The coroner says that he has to draft the inquisition, which must be countersigned by all the members of the jury. He informs the jury that he is writing down the medical cause of death, and that they the jury have concluded that Daniel Evans died of natural causes. He completes the inquisition form, signs it, and passes it to the foreman to countersign. The foreman then passes it on for each member of the jury to sign. This having been done, the coroner says: *"This formally completes the inquest".* He thanks the witnesses and the jury for fulfilling their public duty: *"This is part of the justice system. You have reached a verdict after due consideration and I am very grateful to you."* The jury members file out, and go to claim their expenses.

## Inquest 14
### David Hawkes
### Court 9, Coroner C

This coroner's court is situated in a police station. The court is not signposted or advertised in any way. To gain access, witnesses and family members have to queue up at the police station reception. It is a plain room with chairs laid out in rows, with a desk and chair for the coroner at the front.

This is the first inquest of a morning session. The deceased's two sisters, Denise and Margaret Hawkes, are present. They are accompanied by a social worker who is there not in an official capacity but as a friend and advocate for the sisters. Also present are a police constable, a forensic scientist, a pathologist, and an electrician.

The coroner says that David died six months ago. He had been found dead in his home, and could only be identified by means of dental records because his body was very severely decomposed and in part skeletonised. The coroner summarises David's history. He had been well educated to post-graduate level, but he suffered various mental health problems, never conclusively diagnosed, which led him to live rough and to commit various minor criminal offences. He had been referred to mental health services and there had been attempts to have him 'sectioned' but the psychiatrist concerned had not deemed this to be appropriate. It had been decided that he was not detainable under the terms of the Mental Health Act, but rather that he had a personality disorder. His body was found lying in the bath in an advanced state of decomposition. An electrical cord had been connected to the metal handle of the bath. The Home Office pathologist who had conducted the post mortem had concluded that death was the result of electrocution.

The coroner reviews the purposes of the inquest. He says he will read parts of the statement provided by one of David's sisters. He will call a psychiatrist. He will admit the statements of a neighbour and of the two police officers who attended the scene. He will ask the pathologist not to read his whole report, but to explain key factors contributing to the cause of death. He explains to David's sisters that they can ask any questions "*or you can ask the lady with you to ask those questions on your behalf*".

The coroner then gives a lengthy summary of one sister's statement. As he does this he looks at her frequently, sometimes making statements with an interrogative lilt, implicitly asking her to verify that he is giving an accurate account of what she had written. She responds with occasional nods and muttered affirmatives. The coroner asks if there is anything she wishes to add. She confirms that her brother was mentally ill.

Then we have the evidence of Dr Cooper, David's psychiatrist. It transpires that there is a question mark over whether the mental health services have done all that they could, or should, for David. Dr Cooper had interviewed David on a number of occasions but had declined to 'section' him. He tells the court that David was a heavy drug user, but he was not in need of in-patient care. He addresses some remarks directly to the sisters rather than to the coroner. This encourages them to interject. When did David start taking drugs? The psychiatrist says it was during David's first year at university. He is prepared to elaborate but the coroner brings him to the nub. He asks him to read the specific paragraph of his report that says that detention under Section 2 of the Mental Health Act was not justified. The main thrust of this is that it is very difficult to detain someone like Mr Hawkes against his will – and he was not prepared to enter voluntary institutional care.

The coroner asks the sisters whether they have any questions, but even as he does so he suggests that they may wish to talk to Dr Cooper later. However, the social worker/friend takes the opportunity to ask several rather searching questions. Given Dr Cooper's reservations, the concerns of the family, and evidence of David's self-neglect, was there not a case for a fuller assessment under Section 2 detention? Dr Cooper answers this to the best of his ability – David seemed articulate and sane. It would be a major step to deprive someone of his liberty. The social worker persists: what about David's aggression? What about the very bizarre ways in which he behaved at times? Dr Cooper implies that this behaviour, which he did know about, was due primarily to David's indulgence in drugs. That was not a reason to detain. It had been a difficult decision but David appeared 'together'. The social worker is very persistent on the sisters' behalf. She mentions a series of bizarre incidents. Dr. Cooper answers that although the sisters had told him of this behaviour he did not wish to breach family confidentiality by broaching it with David. David had supplied a rational explanation for what he had done. There was no delusional content.

Other evidence is taken just by way of statement – from the probation report on David; from a neighbour who found him; and from the police officers who discovered the body. It is clear that the coroner is omitting anything too gruesome.

Next to give evidence is the sergeant who was called to the scene. There were no suspicious circumstances, although there was no suicide note. At this point one of the sisters intervenes to ask whether the sergeant had seen David's note – "*Taken over by aliens*". The sergeant confirms that a note to this effect was found in the flat.

Then we have the evidence of the Home Office pathologist. The coroner says "*I don't ask you to read your report, for obvious reasons*". David had been dead for some weeks. The body had been largely skeletonised by bugs. There was no evidence of trauma. After a few exchanges of this nature the coroner apologises to the sisters: "*I am sorry we have to some extent to bring out distasteful, unpleasant evidence. But we don't need to go into it any further*" (said in an interrogative tone).

Then we have a forensic scientist. His conclusion is that this was a "*planned action by Mr Hawkes, resulting in his electrocution*".

Next we have the evidence of an electrician called to the scene. He gives evidence about the way in which the bath had been connected to the electrical supply. When the electrician has given this evidence the coroner emphasises that death would have been instantaneous. He turns to the sisters and asks them whether they have any questions ... "*or is it now, I am afraid, so clear?*" They do not have any more questions.

The coroner summarises the evidence at some length. He emphasises Dr Cooper's conclusion – that there was an insufficient basis on which to support a diagnosis of schizophrenia. David was not detainable under the Mental Health Act. The coroner observes that "'Why?' is not one of those questions I have to answer". But, he says, one does often need to understand the 'why'. He then comes to his verdict. He has to consider suicide, but suicide must not be presumed. There was no note. There was no evidence that David had told anyone that he meant to kill himself. The evidence points in the direction of suicide, but there is no corroboration. "I cannot be certain of his mental condition. Nor can I be satisfied that this was an accident. Given Mr Hawkes's knowledge of electricity, he knew that he would die as a result of the procedure which he had adopted." Then the coroner turns to misadventure – death arising from a deliberate human act that unintentionally had taken a turn that led to death. He cannot be satisfied that that is the right verdict in this case, given Mr Hawkes's understanding of electricity and the steps which he had apparently deliberately taken. The only remaining course open to him is to declare an open verdict, and that is what he does. He does this on the basis that there is insufficient evidence to satisfy any of the other verdicts. The evidence does not fully disclose how it was that the deceased came to kill himself. We know the mechanical means, but not what was in his mind. Was he perhaps experimenting? Did he indeed wish to take his own life? We cannot be completely satisfied of his intention. He addresses the family. "This is not helpful to you, I know, but I hope the exploration of the circumstances has (emphasis) been helpful to you". He thanks the witnesses and expresses his condolences to the family.

When the inquest is closed Dr Cooper goes immediately to talk to the two sisters. They engage him in conversation, which appears to be amicable.

Denise and Margaret Hawkes were interviewed four months after the inquest. Their main concern was that there had been no representation from social services. The family had had a relationship with social services because of David's mental health problems. At the inquest they had wanted to ask questions about the care David had received, and felt thwarted by the absence of a social services representative. They did not blame the coroner for this. Rather they blamed social services and what they saw as their chronic lack of interest in David.

Ruth, the friend who assisted them at the inquest, was a psychiatric social worker who had helped them in the past to understand David's behaviour. The Hawkes felt that there had been a steady decline in David's mental health. They eventually reached a point where they began to be concerned about their personal safety whenever he visited them. He would smash the house up, and they felt he was capable of violence towards them. They described one of his last visits when he had had thrown things, stabbed the walls and furniture with a knife and appeared to threaten Margaret. They came to the decision that they should not let him stay overnight. They lived in continual fear of a visit from him.

As David deteriorated further, the Hawkes became more and more concerned about the lack of action from social services. In March 2000 they wrote a letter to them about David's mental health problems, and their belief that he should be sectioned. They described his bizarre, aggressive and frightening behaviour. Social services did not reply.

The sisters had mixed opinions about the inquest itself. They said they had heard that David's body was partially skeletonised and had been eaten by bugs. One of their chief worries when anticipating the inquest had been that they would have to look at photographs of the body. Margaret had imagined a giant projected photograph on the courtroom wall, showing the partially skeletonised, decomposing David. She said that the inquest *"wasn't as bad as I thought it might be"*. They were very pleased that they had brought Ruth with them. *"She knows the language."* They felt she had a done a good job in representing them. Their main criticism was that the next-of-kin need to know what their rights are. *"Without information you don't know what you can ask."* They would have liked to have seen and read the witness statements beforehand, and known the full details.

Margaret said that she was still not sure that she and her sister knew everything they should know about David's death. *"I felt they shielded us, I was thankful at the time."* But she now regretted this because *"there are still unanswered questions"*, most of them directed at social services. However, the sisters felt that the inquest helped to answer some of their other questions. The coroner seemed professional ... *"he tied things up – he wasn't sloppy"*. They also noted that he was attentive and *"seemed to study our feelings"*. This had impressed them.

The open verdict was a relief. David might have committed suicide, but it might have been an experiment, he was always inventing things. The inquest acknowledged David's problems without saying that he definitely took his own life. The inquest had also helped them with feelings of guilt as to whether they should have let David stay with them in the six months before his death. At the time they had felt unable to prove that David was ill, or a danger to them or himself. The inquest gave a helpful picture of David's state, validating their story.

After the inquest Dr. Cooper had talked to Denise and Margaret. This post-inquest conversation, and the concern and interest of professional witnesses outside the courtroom, had helped them to deal with their feelings of guilt and bereavement. They talked through the absence of a social services representative with Dr. Cooper. *"He offered help if we wanted to take it further."* They said it was unlikely that they would do this. Personal circumstances – their mother's health, and a recent accident – had exhausted them.

## Inquest 15
**Beverley Webster**
**Court 4, Coroner D**

The inquest is held in a small purpose-built courtroom attached to the coroner's office. A coroner's officer brings in a group of eight people – family and friends of the deceased. They include Ralph and Philippa Webster, who are Beverley's children, her brothers and sisters, her mother, and a friend, Natalie. They seem to be in good spirits. Also present is a hospital doctor.

The coroner enters. This is the resumed inquest upon Beverley Webster who died five months ago. The inquest had previously been adjourned in order to gather more evidence. The coroner explains: "*This is not a trial; there are no defendants; and there is no blame to be attached to anyone. We are merely here to ascertain the facts.*"

The coroner calls Ralph Webster, son of the deceased. He is a young man in his late teens or early 20s. At first Ralph appears defensive, but the coroner questions him in such a direct manner, and with such an air of genuine sympathy, that Ralph quickly relaxes and becomes very co-operative. The coroner tells him that he has been very helpful: "*The statement that you made said a lot about your mother. Were you close?*" Ralph replies that they were close, but that they were not in frequent contact. In response to the coroner's leading questions Ralph tells the court that he last saw his mother several months before her death. She had lost weight and looked ill. The coroner observes that Beverley had a history of alcohol and drug abuse. He asks Ralph: "*What did you know about this?*" Ralph answers that his mother had been using drugs for 15 years.

The coroner then calls Philippa Webster. He asks her what drugs her mother took. Philippa replies that her mother took heroin and also other drugs. The coroner then moves on to the events immediately prior to Beverley's death. On leaving a large chainstore she had been manhandled by security guards. After being searched she was arrested and charged with shoplifting. The coroner asks Philippa when she last saw her mother. Philippa says that this was a month before she died. Her mother had been staying with a friend, Natalie.

Natalie is then called to the witness stand. Apparently, at the adjourned inquest there had been a report from a pathologist to the effect that Beverley had died of hypothermia. Accordingly, the coroner begins by asking Natalie whether her house was cold. She replies that her house was not very cold. She says that she had known Beverley for ten years. She knew of her heroin addiction: "*Beverley used drugs every day. She had a methadone script* and she also used street drugs." The coroner asks how Beverley got the money to pay for this. Natalie tells him that Beverley used to shoplift. She was arrested for shoplifting three days before she died. She had been brought to the ground by a rugby tackle from a security guard. This left her with pain in her left shoulder. The shoulder was swollen and discoloured. The next day she went to her GP who told her that her shoulder might be dislocated and sent her for an x-ray. The x-ray was inconclusive, but she was advised that she should keep the shoulder mobile. She was not given pain relief. Natalie continues: "Later that day she was getting more pain. Her arm hurt more and was swollen. I phoned for an ambulance. When the ambulance crew arrived and realised that she was a drug addict, they weren't very nice to her. They pulled her roughly off the bed. Then they took her to hospital. She was returned by ambulance to my house at 5.30 a.m. She was still very ill and cold. The ambulance men that brought her home were so worried about her that they left blankets to warm her up." Because of a family bereavement Natalie had been unable to stay in the house that day … "When I got back, I found that Beverley's arm was going black, and her tongue was numb. I called an ambulance. After that I didn't see her as she was in a high dependency unit."

Next the coroner reads a report from Beverley's GP. Beverley was injecting herself with methadone and heroin. Two days before she died she had attended his surgery, complaining of a painful arm. She had been seen by the practice nurse.

The coroner then reads a report from the local Drug and Alcohol Advisory Service. Beverley had been on a detoxification programme and a rehabilitation programme. However, she had continued to use street drugs.

The coroner says that he should now be calling the doctor from the accident and emergency unit that treated Beverley the first time she went to the hospital. However, this doctor has failed to attend the inquest. A coroner's officer has been trying to get hold of him by telephone. Whilst the coroner's office is still trying to get hold of this doctor, the coroner calls another member of the hospital staff who had treated Beverley when she was admitted for the second time. This doctor explains that Beverley was initially assessed by doctors in A & E, who had then referred her to his medical team. She had first been seen by a senior house officer. At that point she had a low body temperature – low but not dramatically low. She had a swollen right arm. (At this point some family members shake their heads and someone says: "No, it was the other arm".) The doctor ignores this and continues his evidence. He says that Beverley had a low level of oxygen in her blood and she also had a thrombosis that had floated to her lung. This can make someone feel very ill and can even be fatal. The house officer had improved her oxygen level. Beverley was stable, but one has to be wary of clots as they can float off and cause sudden death.

The coroner is aware that some members of the family believe that the doctor has referred to Beverley's right arm, when in fact it was her left that was injured. He asks him to confirm which arm was causing the problem. The doctor repeats that it was the right arm. Some members of the family say again: "*No, it was her left arm*". The doctor checks his notes once more and says very firmly that it was the right arm. He continues with his evidence. He says that Beverley was given antibiotics. This was a difficult procedure because her veins were almost closed down. That was why she was suffering a lot of aches and pains. The medical team also discovered that she had low levels of albumen and was malnourished. She also had kidney problems and was dehydrated. Beverley remained in the accident and emergency department, being monitored by nurses and three doctors.

The doctor continues. He himself first saw Beverley an hour later. This was shortly before she began to deteriorate. She became unconscious, there was no pulse, and her respiration rate was poor. She had to be resuscitated. It was found that her potassium levels were very low. The doctors recognised this to be a symptom of muscle damage. However, it is also a condition that can occur in people who use heroin. The coroner stops the doctor at this point and asks him whether the low potassium level may have been the result of Beverley being crushed by the security guard. The doctor says that this is very unlikely. It would have had to be a very severe injury and in that case one would have expected to see extensive bruising.

The coroner observes that the registered cause of death in Beverley's case was hypothermia. It would seem on this evidence that this was a red herring. What actually killed Beverley was kidney failure as a result of muscle damage, plus the low potassium levels, caused by her drug abuse. The doctor continues with his evidence. He describes the treatment that Beverley received in order to deal with her renal failure.

The coroner then observes that he would like to hear the evidence of the doctor who first saw Beverley in the A & E Department the previous day. He is concerned about the previous admission and the damage to Beverley's shoulder. He asks the doctor who is present whether he would be prepared to discuss this. The doctor is reluctant. He says that it was a coincidence that these various events happened altogether: the injured arm; the thrombosis; and the renal failure. Aches and pains are very common and it would have been hard to anticipate that Beverley was going to experience renal failure.

The coroner is still concerned about the doctor who has failed to attend the inquest. He tells the family that he is going to adjourn for a few minutes in order to make enquiries about his whereabouts. He asks if anyone has any questions. Beverley's mother and daughter both speak up. They are very angry about the treatment that Beverley received on her original admission to the A & E Department. They say that she should not have been sent home at 5 in the morning. They point out that even the ambulance men were worried about her. The coroner says that they are asserting that there has been medical negligence and he warns them that it is not the job of the coroner to pronounce on questions such as that. That is a matter for a different forum. One family member resists this conclusion, observing: "*But the coroner's court is a court of inquiry, and we've all come a long way*". The coroner replies: "*I know, but this is my court*". He leaves the court in order to find out whether any progress has been made in locating the missing doctor.

In the coroner's absence members of the family talk together about Beverley and her encounter with the security guard. Beverley was apparently very small and they mutter that this was indeed a crushing. The coroner enters the courtroom from the rear entrance. He walks over to the family and starts to talk to them. He says that at this point he is addressing them from the floor, and not as a coroner. He talks with them about Beverley being discharged from hospital at 5 o'clock in the morning. He shows them a copy of the hospital doctor's report and tells them that he will give them a copy if they would like one. They answer that they would indeed like this – in fact they would like four copies. He says that he will go and get these photocopied, but he warns them that he cannot give them any other documentation. He then discusses with them the new evidence about Beverley's low potassium level. He says that he was very impressed by the evidence given by the hospital doctor. He observes that this doctor was 'cocky' in his attitude, but that he certainly knew his stuff. He then reflects with the family on the degree of crushing that might have resulted in renal failure. He counsels them against pursuing this line of enquiry and says: "*It is always better if you can put these things behind you and let them go*". To some degree at least the family seems comforted by this exchange. They thank the coroner profusely.

The coroner then leaves the courtroom and reappears on his podium. He tells all and sundry that he is now acting as coroner once again. The missing doctor is apparently on sick leave. The reason that it took so long for the court to find this out was because he had not notified the hospital that he was sick. The coroner observes that the court diary is full for at least six weeks ahead. To adjourn would leave matters hanging in the air, which would be unfair when everyone has come such a long way. He realises that the written medical report does not answer all the questions in the family's mind. Why was Beverley discharged at 5 a.m. in a state that the ambulance men were worried enough to leave blankets? There are other concerns as well. However, he has decided to admit the doctor's written statement as evidence for this inquest. He turns to the coroner's officer and asks her to write a strong letter to the doctor concerned. He checks if the doctor was in fact summoned to attend. It is confirmed that there had been a summons. The coroner turns to the family and says that the doctor can be charged with contempt of court, which could lead to a fine or imprisonment. They give a small cheer. He quietens them down and says that he will require the doctor to attend court and appear before him.

The coroner then moves to his summing up. He states that this has been a very unusual inquest: "*Very rarely as a result of taking a clinical doctor's evidence will we change the cause of death given on a pathologist's report*". He turns to Ralph Webster and thanks him for his frank and helpful evidence. He also thanks the other witnesses. He says: "*Now I can try to establish facts, but not fault. The cause of death was not the damage which arose through Beverley being manhandled, but other causes, as much to do with Beverley's heroin abuse. She had abnormal heart rhythms and the medical team was unable to resuscitate her. I am very grateful to that doctor for his evidence and his explanation. I record that the cause of death was acute renal failure, associated with opiate abuse. There was muscle damage, but I won't use that for my conclusion. Beverley's death was as a result of misadventure: an unforeseen consequence of an action that she herself had taken, either legal or illegal.*"

The coroner addresses the family directly: "*I am fully aware that I have had to balance your needs with the needs of the court. This all happened just before Christmas, which added to the pain. I hope you will be able to remember happier times with Beverley, although these will be clouded by the habit that took her from you. I am sure that her life was different before this. There are so many cases where the pernicious habit of drug-taking ruins people's lives.*"

Members of the family ask the coroner if they will find out what happened to the doctor who failed to attend. The coroner replies that although he knows that they are interested, this is actually no concern of theirs. The coroner leaves his podium but once more re-enters the courtroom through the side door. He advises the family on how to register Beverley's death, and gives them copies of the documents that he had promised.

# RDS Publications

## Requests for Publications

Copies of our publications and a list of those currently available may be obtained from:

Home Office
Research, Development and Statistics Directorate
Communication Development Unit
Room 275, Home Office
50 Queen Anne's Gate
London SW1H 9AT
Telephone:    020 7273 2084 (answerphone outside of office hours)
Facsimile:    020 7222 0211
E-mail:       publications.rds@homeoffice.gsi.gov.uk

alternatively

why not visit the RDS website at
          Internet: http://www.homeoffice.gov.uk/rds/index.html

where many of our publications are available to be read on screen or downloaded for printing.